CW01512874

AIR MARSHAL SIR KEITH PARK

My thanks to Wendy Rowlands, to whom the completion of this book owes much

AIR MARSHAL SIR KEITH PARK

VICTOR OF THE BATTLE OF BRITAIN, DEFENDER OF MALTA

MURRAY ROWLANDS

Pen & Sword
AVIATION

First published in Great Britain in 2021 by
PEN AND SWORD AVIATION
An imprint of
Pen & Sword Books Limited
Yorkshire – Philadelphia

Copyright © Murray Rowlands, 2021

ISBN 978 1 52676 790 5

The right of Murray Rowlands to be identified as Author
of this work has been asserted by him in accordance with the Copyright,
Designs and Patents Act 1988.

A CIP catalogue record for this book is available from the British Library.

All rights reserved. No part of this book may be reproduced or transmitted in any
form or by any means, electronic or mechanical including photocopying, recording
or by any information storage and retrieval system, without permission from the
Publisher in writing.

Typeset in Ehrhardt 11/14 by
SJmagic DESIGN SERVICES, India.
Printed and bound in the UK by TJ Books Ltd.

Pen & Sword Books Limited incorporates the imprints of Atlas, Archaeology,
Aviation, Discovery, Family History, Fiction, History, Maritime, Military, Military
Classics, Politics, Select, Transport, True Crime, Air World, Frontline Publishing,
Leo Cooper, Remember When, Seaforth Publishing, The Praetorian Press,
Wharncliffe Local History, Wharncliffe Transport, Wharncliffe True Crime and
White Owl.

For a complete list of Pen & Sword titles please contact
PEN & SWORD BOOKS LIMITED
47 Church Street, Barnsley, South Yorkshire S70 2AS, United Kingdom
E-mail: enquiries@pen-and-sword.co.uk
Website: www.pen-and-sword.co.uk

Or
PEN AND SWORD BOOKS
1950 Lawrence Rd, Havertown, PA 19083, USA
E-mail: Uspen-and-sword@casematepublishers.com
Website: www.penandswordbooks.com

Contents

CONTENTS

Foreword

Air Chief Marshal Sir Keith Park is one of New Zealand's greatest military leaders. Murray Rowlands' thoughtful biography, *Air Marshal Sir Keith Park*, will introduce a new generation of readers to an outstanding commander who played an absolutely central role in winning the Battle of Britain in 1940.

This biography contains significant new information and insights into both Park's professional career and his personal life. He was a remarkably self-contained man with great reserves of inner strength and willpower. These traits helped him through professional crises as well as personal tragedies.

Keith Park was a very modern commander who fully appreciated how all elements of an armed force must work effectively together to produce optimal outcomes. Throughout his military career, which saw him leave New Zealand in 1915 as a Corporal in the New Zealand Expeditionary Force and return in 1948 as a much decorated retired Air Chief Marshal, Park remained an undemonstrative, modest man who led by example. He respected all those with ability, loyalty and a willingness to work hard. He had, however, no time for the lax or incompetent, especially those who failed the men and women under their command. Park was, as Murray Rowlands points out, at his best in war. In crisis after crisis during the Second World War he displayed leadership of the highest order. Keith Park had a great ability to analyse complex problems and then work out and implement successful responses.

During the Second World War few individuals did more than Sir Keith Park to defend and uphold the values of freedom and justice that lie at the heart of the national psyche of both the United Kingdom and New Zealand. Murray Rowlands' *Air Marshal Sir Keith Park* makes this clear and sets out the debt we owe him.

Kevin Short, Air Marshal
Chief of Defence Force
Wellington
NEW ZEALAND
August 2020

Preface

When Sir Keith Park's name is mentioned in relation to the Battle of Britain it is more often than not greeted with a blank stare. This is despite the fact that in 2009 after a campaign a statue was raised to him in Central London.

It is now eleven years since this happened, and the 80th anniversary of the Battle of Britain is with us. Publications now recognise Park as being the architect of victory and yet the memory of his contribution seems to have faded. I hope my book will remedy this.

Vincent Orange's biography of Park was published in 1984 and could not benefit from a whole range of historians' reappraisals of events which happened during those months in 1940. Nevertheless Dr Orange has acted as a crucial pathfinder through the course of Park's life. I am also indebted to Christer Bergström for providing a clear picture of what the Luftwaffe was doing as it prepared its attacks on Britain. His book provides balance to the picture of the conflict in the skies of Britain.

I was very fortunate to be able to draw on the extensive collection of books on aircraft at Farnborough Library and the guidance and help I received from library staff. Thanks also to the staff at the Imperial War Museum and the Wigram Museum in Christchurch New Zealand

This is a political story which crosses eighty years and covers the treatment of Dowding and Park at the moment of victory in November 1940. Those who conspired in this shoddy act operated in the shadow of two great men.

Murray Rowlands

Chapter 1

Starting from the Lowest Level

It would require a feat of the imagination to conceive of a less propitious background for a man who would be the genius behind the first victory for the Allies in the Second World War.

In 1867 Europeans were drawn to a beautiful part of the North Island of New Zealand, south of Auckland, by the discovery of gold in the Kuranui Stream on the Coromandel Peninsula. The resulting gold rush resulted in the creation of the town of Thames which was an amalgam of two settlements, Grahamstown and Shortland, which became known as the Shotover and produced 102,353 ounces of bullion in its lifetime. In the period 1868 to 1871 the Thames mines officially produced 2,327,619 ounces of gold, which would today be worth US$3,000 million.

It was not gold that first brought John Livingstone Park to New Zealand. Like so many of the original settlers arriving in the country his first venture was into sheep farming. This was despite having originally moved from his home town of Aberdeen to study mining at the Royal School of Mines in London. Combining an interest in mountaineering and geology, in 1889 he became Director of the Thames School of Mines relegating climbing to a leisure activity. He had married Frances Rogers in Wellington and they were to have ten children: seven daughters and three boys. Keith, born in 1892, was the ninth child. His earliest memories were of the giant machines crushing the ore to remove its gold. The family lived in Totara just south of Thames in a two-storey building on the Thames side of the local cemetery overlooking the Kauaeranga valley. Keith attended a number of schools in the town, one of which was Tararu just north of the town.

The family moved away from the gold face to Birkenhead, which was then becoming a prosperous suburb of Auckland with a sugar refinery and orchards. Young Park was enrolled for King's College, an all-male school with a strong Anglican ethos which was to remain with him throughout his life. However he was a poor scholar, preferring to frequent the ferry wharf on Waitemata Harbour and developing a strong interest in things nautical, which was to provide a recreational outlet throughout his life.

In 1891 his father secured a post as Professor of Mining at Otago University, travelling south to another community built around gold discovered in Central Otago. This coincided with an episode in his family involving his mother leaving and moving to Australia. For a woman to do this and face the difficulties of an independent life for a separated woman with the prejudices of colonial society poses a whole series of unanswered questions. Her early death in March 1916 in Australia is not commented on in Dr Orange's biography of Park. Clearly indicated is that his father had to adopt a patriarchal role in taking responsibility for his family who now moved to Dunedin in the South Island. One can only surmise about the effect of this on Park as he began studying at Otago Boys' High School in 1906.

The loss of a mother may explain Park's self-sufficiency and ability to submerge himself in things military. This was encouraged by a visit of Lord Kitchener to his school in 1909 which was augmented by a strong interest in guns and horses coupled with the jingoism associated with the Empire following the Boer War even in this far flung part of Empire. Park joined the Territorial Army which had been organised by General Godley who was to lead the New Zealand Expeditionary Force when war broke out in 1914. He had been an active member of the cadets at his school, perhaps as some compensation for a poor scholastic record.

But it was his other interest in things nautical which led him to join The Union Steam Ship Company, as a beanpole of a boy of 6 foot 5 at 19. Travel by sea was a crucial factor in New Zealand with even the journey between the North and South Islands sometimes being hazardous. As a purser, Keith Park dressed in his white jacket would serve passengers in the lounge as well as caring for them in their cabins. He started working on vessels plying the New Zealand coastline and graduated to those servicing Australia and the Pacific. His success was indicated by a rapid rate of promotion well beyond what might have been expected for someone of his age.

Park's Territorial Army experience in the Field Artillery and the fact that many of his friends were enlisting meant that rather than joining the navy he opted to enlist with the New Zealand army. He enlisted in the Field Artillery commencing duty on 14 December 1914 and was promoted to corporal on 1 February 1915. This was to be a crucial event in his life, taking him away from New Zealand from 1915 to 1923. He would not see in those eight years James his father, someone better respected than loved, from whom Dr Orange suggests he inherited the virtues of resilience and abstention.

Early settlement on Coromandel Goldfield, Park's birthplace.

Steamship Maori on which Park served as a purser.

Above: New Zealand troops landing at Gallipoli.

Left: Park with First World War decorations.

Chapter 2

The First Taste of Warfare

In February 1915 Park left New Zealand as a corporal in the Howitzer Battery. Fifty years later Park recalled the travails of this novice army on landing at Suvla Bay on the Gallipoli Campaign: 'We had never fired the gun before. We were so short of ammunition that we had not been allowed to expend any in training… We had just 2 shells per day.' His attitude towards the British High Command originated from his experience on Gallipoli. Park saw the General in charge of the landings, Sir William Birdwood, dancing across the beach for his daily swim. He realised that it was possible to relax and still retain the respect of the men he led. There was no necessity to stick to the letter of the rule book to achieve military success working with men who had been turned from civilians to soldiers. In contrast Sir Aylmer Hunter-Watson, the Commander of the 29th Division, illustrated to Park the danger of approaching the management of men under his command in an over-formal manner when he inspected Park's battery shortly after some of the men had over-indulged on rum. In desperation the seriously drunk men were placed on stretchers and told to pose as being dead. Hunter-Watson leant over the stretchers and in his best sepulchral voice said, 'I salute the dead,' much to the derision of the soldiers.

By July Park had been promoted to second lieutenant in the New Zealand Army. He then made the decision to switch to the British Army, becoming a member of the Royal Horse and Field Artillery. He had served 264 days in the New Zealand Army. On 24 September Park joined the 10th Battery, 147th Brigade Royal Field Artillery. On Gallipoli, conditions were appalling. It was the beginning of a jaundiced view of the British Army's organizational skills which was to stay with him throughout his military career. At the same time he carefully observed the skills associated with the more able leaders at Gallipoli, such as attention to detail, regular tours of inspection, and indifference to danger. Some of these leaders he dismissed as pompous 'hot air merchants'. He took with him the lessons of the disaster at Gallipoli when planning campaigns in the Mediterranean in the Second World War.

By January 1916 Park was back at Suez in Egypt and had become aware of the important role aircraft would play in the conduct of modern war. He made a request to fly over a battlefield, which was contemptuously refused by an officer who dismissed aircraft as having no value. He was to find this attitude towards the use of aircraft for observation of artillery positions only too common. No provision was made in his experience of training at Suez for the growing importance of aircraft in the battles being fought.

The order came through on 21 February to prepare to go to France, which was a relief because his men lacked decent tropical kit. His battery travelled to Alexandria and then by horse transport to Marseille, finally arriving there on 17 March. His 29th Division was ordered to travel to the Somme on cattle trucks, reaching the Somme on 21 March dirty, frozen and hungry. In driving rain his battery moved ten miles to Vauchelles, both horses and men being covered in mud in the process. Park then had one of the many accidents that plagued his military career when he was thrown from a horse which then proceeded to fall on him.

Park recalls as a nightmare, mud and inadequate preparation for an attack due to commence on 1 July. Despite seasoned troops emphasising the necessity for concealment from observation aircraft, this advice was ignored. However, significantly, Park was given permission to accompany a pilot from 8 Squadron on a flight observing the strategic position of his brigade's gun positions. This revealed how the paths made by the guns in the earth were clearly visible, making any attempt to disguise their presence useless. By 5 July, Park's battery was moved to a new position, this coinciding with his suffering badly from malaria and being hospitalised till 4 August. Finally on 6 September his brigade was sent to a position near the Menin Gate on the Ypres Salient. It was here that Park overheard some of his men praising the role of the Royal Flying Corps in being able to effectively respond to attacks by enemy artillery.

On 21 October 1916 he was working with his horses seeking to withdraw one of his few remaining guns for repair when a shell exploded under his horse. Following a hazardous and difficult journey Park was repatriated to England. Despite a ban on serving soldiers joining the Royal Flying Corps, Park somehow managed to pull strings effectively and accomplished a transfer to the RFC. He had to endure the derision from some of his fellow officers for withdrawing from the 'real war'. Behind him were two years in artillery, and before him were thirty years as an aviator, fighter pilot and air commander.

Above: Royal Flying Corps trainees receiving instruction.

Right: Squadron Leader Park.

A Bristol F.2 Fighter – one of the aircraft on which Park built up his reputation as an ace

Scene at Bertangles in France where Park was based.

Chapter 3

The Making of a Fighter Pilot

While working as an instructor at Woolwich Armoury in December 1916, Park's physical condition had led to him being classified as unfit to ride a horse. He managed to overcome this for acceptance into the Royal Flying Corps, a crucial development in Park's life, as well as coinciding with major developments in warfare that by 1940 would put in question the survival of Britain.

Park commented years later: 'It may seem strange that I was considered unfit to ride a horse but fit to fly an aeroplane. But tradition was strong in those days of horse-drawn artillery and an officer and gentleman was expected to ride into battle on a charger.' His recruitment on 9 December 1916 coincided with instructions that all new recruits to the Royal Flying Corps should follow a designated period of instruction called the Gosport System and that there should be no recruitment to the RFC without prior training.

In fact transfer from other parts of the services from this time became very dependent on the state of the air war, and officers seeking to transfer to the RFC were only considered if they had previous flying experience. From 1916 a pilot's licence, known as 'the ticket', was required.

The rate of casualties on the Somme after July 1916 and the demand for pilots meant that recruitment policy had to change. The RFC that Park joined was known as 'the suicide club' because of the death rate amongst pilots on the Western Front. As well as a more practical attitude towards the skills needed, from 1917 emphasis was placed on the necessary psychology of the cadet to become a pilot. Park was helped by the applicant interview, which emphasised attitude more than 'obscure' medical matters.

In November 1916 he received the following joining instructions: 'You will report to the Air Ministry in service dress drill order. Civilian shoes, coloured scarves, fur collars and other irregularities will not be worn on duty or on leave. You must be available in London when you report to the Air Ministry so you can collect your uniform within 30 minutes of receiving your orders.'

Park's dispatch to the RFC training school in Reading was the beginning of a period of training for pilots he was to become so critical of in 1941. At Reading in early 1917 he would find a training curriculum which bore little relevance to the skills required of a fighter pilot. For instance it included detailed instruction on how to mend a Lewis gun, an activity which would be impossible while piloting an aeroplane. There was nothing about the mechanics of flight.

His routine at Reading was a 6 am wake-up call followed by inspection on parade. The day consisted of two lectures on aerial warfare and two on practical issues relating to flight with the day finishing at 4 pm. The written exam he was to take was considered 'easy', perhaps recognising that there was an increasing demand for men coming out of the Western Front. In some cases the course was arbitrarily cut short. On graduation Park was given £50 to purchase a uniform and pay of 7 shillings and 6 pence a day. Once he was a recognised pilot this became 1 pound 4 shillings and 6 pence plus 6 shillings as a daily allowance.

After this Park moved to Netheravon on Salisbury Plain. Here training involved practical experience in a Maurice Farnham MF11 known as a Shorthorn. It was an aircraft considered dangerously underpowered, with the propensity to stall at only 5 mph less than its top speed. It was called a 'rumpeter' because of the sound of its engine and resembled a Victorian bathtub. Park was flying with an instructor as soon as he arrived at Netheravon. Very little instruction could take place in flight – the instructor had to kick Park's seat to attract his attention; hence learning to fly was 'by the seat of the trainee's pants'. Instruction concentrated mainly on the skills required to land and take off, and because of the weaknesses in the aircraft's performance was only possible in near perfect weather. When Park achieved his first solo flight, his instructor immediately asked him to repeat it again. To graduate as a pilot he had to prove he could fly a service aeroplane satisfactorily, carry out a cross-county flight, safely land in two places, climb to 8,000 feet, land with his engine stopped within a 50 foot radius and make two landings with the aid of flares in the dark. He qualified for his wings by achieving thirty hours flying in a service aeroplane. Reconnaissance and combat were not taught before pilots were sent to France.

Park was more fortunate than most of his contemporary cadets in that in March 1917 he was posted to Rendcomb near Cirencester as an instructor; an indication of some skill and a shortage of experienced pilots available to work in this capacity. This meant he could accumulate 135 flying hours before being posted to France; considerably more than other cadets who were thrust into the conflict where life expectation for new pilots was less than a week.

There was some indication of management failures, for when he arrived at the RFC base at Boulogne he was told that he was to be a bomber pilot rather than a fighter pilot and he was posted to the pool of pilots at the base at St Omer in that capacity. The base home to four squadrons was next to the racecourse where pilots were trained in the important observation skills needed for artillery. However, on his own initiative he made contact with 48 Squadron following the frustration of cooling his heels and not flying for some weeks.

He was entering a period of clear German superiority where Germany enjoyed a 2 to 1 advantage in kills in aerial conflict. Fortunately Park arrived just at the time when the Bristol fighter was replacing other inadequate aeroplanes faced with superior German models. A major advance was that instead of just one gun operated by the observer, a second was added at the front operated by the pilot. Park moved to an airfield close to Dunkirk where his marksmanship and cool head in inevitable crisis associated with aerial conflict quickly revealed itself. It was here that Park began to learn the requirements of successful fighter conflict.

The Allies were able to produce aircraft at a higher rate than the Germans and by 1918 this was a vital element in the final victory. Park had learned this lesson which he brought to bear in his relationship with Lord Beaverbrook, the Director of Aircraft Production during the Battle of Britain, when the production of aircraft to replace losses was equally vital.

Joshua Levine of Park's 48 Squadron recalls the instruction he received from Major Park: 'Our orders were to go as low as possible and concentrate on shooting up German troops or any other worthwhile targets. The Brisfit [Bristol F2 fighter] being a two-seater was much larger than the scout machine and had a bigger wingspan and was not built for low flying. I cannot remember how many machines I flew were put out of action by fire from ground troops. The mechanics and riggers worked non-stop at this time. Major Park inspired us all with his calm certainty that we would win through, although he hated sending us out on these near suicide missions. So we soldiered on.'

Park was respected in his willingness to discuss aspects of the conflict with all those involved in the fighting. He was to employ this approach with his pilots in the Battle of Britain. In the summer of 1917 he patrolled the Channel in search of returning German Gotha bombers who were attacking London; he was never able to locate them. This experience provided lessons he was to use to support the evacuation of Dunkirk in 1940.

Until 15 September 1917 Park achieved twenty-six days of successful destruction of enemy aircraft, this coinciding with the award of the Distinguished Service Order. However, Trenchard insisted he should be awarded a Bar to the Military Cross he had already won. In the citation it was stated, 'He has at all times set an example of dash and tenacity.' Among Park's victims at this time were leading German aces such as Hauptmann Otto Hartmann, the Commanding Officer of Jasta 28, who had seven Allied kills to his credit, and the stepson of General Ludendorff, Franz Pernet, a member of the famous unit Jasta Boelke. Reports note Park's dash and the fortitude he manifested against the considerable odds he encountered. On 27 September he was awarded the Croix de Guerre for conspicuous service in Flanders.

On 21 March 1918 Park took over his first command, which coincided with the German offensive. He was faced with a high attrition rate among his pilots and the vulnerability of newly qualified men who had to be thrown into the fray, as well as a retreat with airfields being overrun. The task of the RFC in the Spring Offensive was to improve the effectiveness of Allied artillery fire. Park realised how little time in training was devoted to achieving this. The ability to respond was hindered by bad weather. During this time 48 Squadron's activities involved non-stop reconnaissance behind enemy lines, attacking specific targets using machine guns and primitive bombs, and providing intelligence of German movements.

The RFC was seriously hampered by Allied communication systems failing when the artillery batteries with whom the spotter planes were meant to communicate lost their wireless sets and antennas in the retreat. He received instructions from Major General Salmond, someone who became a significant figure in his later career, to concentrate on attacking everything his pilots could see on the enemy's side of the line. Foch, the Supreme Commander, demanded incessant attack. But although the tide was beginning to run in the Allies' favour, the Germans were still capable of retaliation. On 24 August five Gotha bombers made an attack on 48 Squadron at Bertangles causing major damage which Jack Slessor, his senior commander, believed would put his squadron out of action for some weeks. In fact, the squadron's Bristols were flying again in two days. Despite being badly wounded himself he carried some of his injured men from the burning hangers.

Some idea of how the rapidly developing RFC was regarded by the army and navy at the time is given by General Haig: 'These aviators of ours are the biggest liars in the world. Cocky fellows impossibly claiming impossible achievements. What proof can they give of their preposterous tales? They only go into the air service because they haven't the pluck to serve in the infantry.'

But who were these aces, whose numbers Park joined in 1917? About five per cent of combat pilots accounted for more than half of air victories. Originally Park would have been classified as a 'star turn' – words inherited from show business. The Germans referred to them as *Überkanonen* – 'top guns'. There was a reluctance at first by the War Office, indeed a failure, to recognise the bravery of the fighter, bomber and reconnaissance crews. However, the media's coverage of the war quickly fastened onto the value of recognising aces.

While the introduction of the Bristol aircraft proved such a success later in the war, there were teething problems with its guns jamming and the supply of poor-quality ammunition; moreover, it was extremely vulnerable at low altitude.

Park had also to work with the dangerous and still developing skills associated with taking aerial photographs of the enemy's trenches. Real skill was required to produce an effective plate; the pilot having to change the plate on the camera in freezing conditions and to steady the plane to avoid vibration, all the while being shot at from the ground and from the air. By 1918 a long-nosed camera had been developed able to take a larger picture.

During this time Park himself survived a number of forced landings, escaping relatively unscathed. In the evenings he and his pilots would sing songs, often with black humour such as this one the RFC had composed:

The Dying Airman

The young aviator lay dying,
And in the wreckage he lay,
To his comrades gathered round him,
These last parting words he did say.
Take the cylinder out of my kidneys
The connecting rod out of my brain
From the small of my back take the crankshaft
And assemble the engine again.

As well as these convivial links with his men Park insisted on maintaining a relationship with the ground crew who were servicing his aeroplanes.

As always with so-called kills there is a dispute of the actual figure attributed to Park as an ace but at the end of the war he could be reliably credited with at least 11 aeroplanes shot down and another 13 damaged.

With the Armistice, Park was able to reflect on what he had learned about aerial combat from 1917 to late 1918. In 1922 he was to produce a paper on this subject. Firstly airfield and bases should not be clustered. He noted that even after bombing it should be possible to return an airfield to operations quickly. His second point was that specialist low-flying planes were required for strafing and that larger planes were not suitable for this. Thirdly there was the question of the role escorting fighter planes would play with bombers; this was to become an important issue in the Battle of Britain. Fourthly he was very aware just how much the theory and practice of aerial warfare had been devised on the hoof during the war. It was vital that this be worked on more methodically at institutions like the Staff College which was opened in 1922.

When the First World War ended, Keith Park was a member of an air force incomparably the strongest in the world. There were 30,000 officers, 261,175 men, 22,647 aircraft of all kinds, and 103 airships (a combat strength of 3,300 aircraft). There were 274 aerodromes overseas, which in the inter-war period became part of the process of imperial policing. In Britain many of the 401 aerodromes would again be used when war was declared in 1939. Park's 48 Squadron was part of the 99 on the Western Front, while there were 14 in the Middle East, 4 in Italy, 16 in the Mediterranean and about 200 attached to training squadrons.

Park indicates that even at Gallipoli in 1915 he had set his eyes on entering the RFC even though the officers around him were referring to it as a 'ragtime show'. Park writes about the disorganization he found in 1917 after arriving in Boulogne and finding himself in a pilots' pool where the expectation was that he should be able to fly planes he had never flown before.

After a period of unemployment, on his own initiative he contacted 48 Squadron, a fighter squadron. He pointed out that small aerodromes were hazardous to primitive planes on landing and were often manned by offensive officers. From his New Zealand egalitarian background he contrasts this with uncomplaining ground crew often expected to work fourteen-hour days and yet maintaining a level of considerable enthusiasm.

Here was the practice of allocating new recruits the oldest machines and on these required to prove their competence. Because of a general shortage of machines for practice new pilots and observers were sent out on patrol about a week later. He asks a vital rhetorical question why these new pilots' survival rate was so low, and highlights a lack of experience in formation flying – for which there was no training at all, no experience of flying at high altitudes and a complete lack of knowledge of aerial combat. There were no local systems of briefing within the base about the area to be patrolled, the height at which they would be flying on patrol – everything appeared to be decided on the spur of the moment.

Park found in practice that combat with the Luftwaffe seldom conformed with the concept of formation flying. Invariably combat took the form of a disorganised dogfight where the result was determined by a combination of luck and skill. The pilots who came to be in his charge divided into those who were good offensive fighters and those who were less aggressive but were able to take reconnaissance photos. As in the bitter winter of 1940, Park observed in 1917 that fatigue among his men was often associated with the tension related to long periods on standby.

At the end of 1917 he went back to England on leave and took advantage of a course on Avro planes and the means to improve training.

His arrival back at Bertangles on 1 March 1918 coincided with Operation Michael, a major attack by the Germans on the Western Front. His orders were to do all in his power to stem this advance through bomb and machine gun fire together with detailed scrutiny of back areas.

By April conditions around Amiens had stabilised and his squadron could be organised into reconnaissance, back area photography and escort duty. During 1918 he reported that casualties were heavier than 1917 due to the adoption of a more aggressive approach to escort duties.

Park believed that fighter reconnaissance pilots should receive equivalent training to scout pilots and be a good type. He said there existed no proven tactics for aerial fighting but ascendancy was gained through courage and dash. At the same time there was a need for tactics to be sorted out on the ground and not be subject to ad hoc decisions once planes were airborne.

Park was always aware of technological change and even by the end of the war was examining the role radio technology would play in wartime aviation. As well as this he closely observed the physical consequences of flying at high altitudes, being around 16,000 feet, which resulted in pilot fatigue and many reporting unfit. By the end of the war Park had judged that new pilots needed about 4 or 5 months' flying time to be really effective.

Chapter 4

Peacetime

The first months after the war brought difficulties, with the Air Ministry deciding that among the ninety per cent of demobilised personnel from the RAF, Park should not be eligible to be on the pay roll. Further, his application to Christchurch for employment in the embryonic New Zealand air industry was rejected in favour of a candidate who could offer engineering skills. However, by August 1919 he had been offered a permanent commission as a flight lieutenant. At Hawkinge, surplus aircraft engines were being sent to be dumped in the sea, but despite this, by 1 February he was commander of the only fighter squadron in the country.

One event in Park's life was possibly more important than the Armistice on 11 November 1918: his marriage to Dorothy Parish, something of a society beauty, on 25 November at Christ Church Ludgate by the Bishop of Hull. It must have been a picture book wedding with the tall Park and lovely Dorothy, known in the family as Dol. She was from a well-to-do background, used to the care of servants, but her introduction to married life was rented rooms and transport via a sidecar attached to her husband's motorcycle.

She had married someone with an uncertain future, with the government about to begin a massive reduction of the air force it had created during the war. Coupled to this she had to cope with her new husband's health as the legacy of Gallipoli and the Somme caught up with him – and her nursing experience was required. Not only did RAF command look sceptically at Park's health in relation to his continued employment, but the posts on offer required frequent moves in a shrinking air force.

In Dol, Keith discovered an opposite able to compensate for his somewhat austere personality. She loved company and, coming from a sophisticated background, was able to assist her husband develop the social graces he needed as his career progressed. For the fifty years of their marriage, she was an abundant source of good advice.

PEACETIME

The question facing the country and one which dominated the newly formed RAF with direct consequence for Park was how much air power should be retained and modernised? *The Aeroplane* magazine in an editorial spoke of heavy gloom. In 1920 the RAF budget was limited to £15 million and of this only six home squadrons were to be retained together with two training groups. The editorial advanced the case that command of the air had now become more important than command of the sea. An article in the aeronautical press suggested that only ten per cent of those currently in the Royal Air Force would be able to remain after demobilisation. It was suggested that the clever and keen would be lured away, with the officers becoming racing car drivers or even car salesman. For the NCOs there would be opportunities driving buses or steam rollers. The fate of ground staff mechanics would be to assemble sewing machines, sharpening razors in barbers' shops and seeking jobs in tin can factories. A suggested opportunity for the skilled riggers maintaining contemporary aeroplanes would be twisting the hay ropes for farmers.

When scores of companies who supplied the RAF were now closing due to the drying up of orders, Park's success in retaining employment indicates there was some recognition of the unique skills and competences he had to offer in a difficult post-war environment. The idea of disbanding the RAF and integrating it with the army and navy was being canvassed. Churchill

Officer trainees at course at Andover. Park is in the back row second on the right.

prevented this by reappointing Sir Hugh Trenchard as Chief of Air Staff with the new role of aerial policeman of the Empire in parts of the world such as Iraq.

In April 1920 Park used his weekend away from a posting to Andover airfield in Hampshire to co-pilot a flight in a plane uncannily named *Last days for a flight around Britain*. The large plane had a crew of 2 pilots, 2 navigators, 2 wireless operators and 3 engine fitters. It took them 28 hours to circumnavigate Britain, some 1,880 miles. It came as a surprise in later years to discover Park's role in this pioneering flight, but in the interwar years it was necessary for the survival and development of aviation to have activities such as this before the public. Park was to play an important role in the air tournaments that took place throughout the interwar years, such as the one at Hendon in 1920. On the instruction of Sholto Douglas, someone who would have a considerable impact on Park's later career, he organised a flypast of three 4-engine Handley Page V/1500 bombers. Sholto Douglas and a pilot called MacFarlane flew one each, providing what *The Aeroplane* describes as a terrifying sensation by passing just fifteen feet above the audience. This resulted in a stern rebuke from Trenchard.

Throughout this period Park grappled with ill health and the possibility of being invalided out of the RAF. However, in May 1923, still thin and anaemic, he and Dol sailed to the Aboukir air base in Egypt for him to take up an appointment as a technical officer. Although Park was at home in Egypt, his senior officers expressed concern about his fitness to fly. In contrast, comments were placed on his file about him being a very fine officer.

Park returned to Britain in 1926 and was offered a post on the staff of Air Marshal Sir John Salmond in recognition of the practical understanding and skills he could bring to the formulation of air defence policy. Key elements towards this were beginning to emerge, including a chain of command involving army, navy and civilian cooperation. Picking up on the scientist Watson-Watt's experimental work, support for the development of early warning systems, including rapid communication systems on the ground and between aircraft, were brought into practice. Park moved to Uxbridge coinciding with the development of searchlights and the recruiting of air attack observers. He was responsible for Operations, Intelligence, Mobilization and Combined Training; his was a senior position in relation to the three other squadron leaders and he occupied fourth place in a hierarchy which included Sir John Salmond, Holt and Wing Commander J.S.T. Bradley.

PEACETIME

By 1929 Park had become responsible for organising the flying pageants at Hendon, which drew 132,000 spectators in July. These were occasions when newly developed aircraft were tested in the form of King's Cup air races. It would not have been lost on Park that at the same time at Calshot a Supermarine 5.5 was flown much faster than anything flying at Hendon.

On 21 June 1931 he was back at Hendon, marking the arrival home of a Vickers 146 Vivid that had flown to Warsaw and returned on the same day. The RAF display he helped to organise was attended by 170,000 spectators. This together with his appointment as Station Commander at Northolt in January 1931 brought him further to the attention of decision makers at the Air Ministry with his responsibility for the flights of senior Air Ministry staff and the Prime Minister himself.

He then moved to take charge of one of the University Air Training Centres at Oxford in September 1932, as Chief Instructor, achieving an honorary MA for his work, while registering 917 flying hours. Together with R.P. Don from Cambridge he wrote to the Air Ministry complaining about moves to militarise the civilian nature of the University Air Squadrons. However, by 1937 graduates from this training were automatically receiving commissions facilitating their movement into the RAF Voluntary Reserve. In 1939 with the outbreak of war these squadrons were disbanded.

There now followed a period from 1934 to 1936 when Park was appointed to a British Air Attaché post in Argentina involving a strange mixture of diplomat and salesman skills. Dol's family usefully had a connection to the country. On 3 November Dol and he left for Buenos Aires, leaving their sons Ian and Colin in boarding schools. Over the next months he travelled through Latin America observing the dominance of the American aircraft industry and noting the limitations of domestic aircraft industries in countries like Venezuela and Chile. The best that the Argentinian domestic air industry could achieve was a training biplane. He caustically observed why this might be the case: 'The officers spend too much time strutting about with swords on when they should be either attending lectures or carrying out flying training.'

Chapter 5

The 30s – The Prelude

Major General Sir Sefton Brancker put forward his reservations about the ability of the League of Nations to make war a thing of the past in post war Europe: 'The restrictions of the development of Germany's aerial strength are drastic on paper but count for little in practice; indeed, they are likely to act as a stimulant to ingenuity and national organization once the country has returned to normal conditions.'

This proved an accurate prophecy, with gliders apparently not restricted by the Versailles Treaty becoming aircraft. With the declining political situation in Europe and particularly Hitler's rise to power in 1933 the development of new aircraft such as the Hawker Hurricane became a priority. The challenge faced by Air Marshal Dowding's team, which now included Park, set up at Bentley Priory, was to work towards an integrated scheme of fighter defence. Technical advances such as the development of wing flaps and lighter radios were emerging, but from 1934 producing guns with the ability to pierce the steel shell of bombers became essential. Park had joined Dowding to augment his methodological plans commenced in the late 1920s to develop fighter defence.

The armament manufacturer Vickers was to find a new role. As reported in *The Aeroplane*: 'In all previous revolutions in transport there had been a period of preparation, of gradual evolution during which surrounding circumstances accommodated themselves little by little to the new factor without sudden change. The plane is the linear successor to the railway, the bicycle, and the car.'

Keith Park had been identified since the First World War as being a commander with special ability by Dowding, and so to some extent he achieved a senior position within Fighter Command on Dowding's coat tails. 'Stuffy' Dowding had been given Bentley Priory in Stanmore as his headquarters in 1926. Before its establishment as Fighter Command Headquarters there were discussions about how the space designated as the command centre should be organised. Based on his First World War experience, Park supported the view that all intelligence sources, from intelligence, radar stations and observation, should be carefully plotted. Only then would it be transmitted to the defence groups being set up around the country. The ballroom at Bentley Prior became the operations room for the Battle of Britain, dominated by a large map covering Edinburgh in the north, to the French coast, and from the border of Wales in the west, to the east of Belgium. On the map could be shown as many aircraft movements, friendly and hostile, for which as much intelligence had been gathered as possible. This was supplemented by a system of lights indicating the readiness of aircraft for combat.

Reviewing the progress towards an effective means of defence against bomber attack, Air Commodore Probert pointed to the damage that retrenchment of spending on the Royal Air Force had caused in the 1920s. The whole challenge was how to survive in such an atmosphere of retrenchment. The prevailing analysis presented to Dowding and Park was that the threat would come from France towards the south-east of England. An early perception of this threat and advocacy of where airfields should be located was to prove of great importance in 1940. From practical experience they proved to be in the right place. Probert claims that much work on fighter defence happened almost in spite of politicians. There was a prevailing belief, based on the Gotha attacks on London in the First War, that the bomber would always get through. A dominant idea was that deterrence through counter-attack was only replaced in 1938/9 by the advent of the Hurricane, the Spitfire and radar. According to Dr Orange it was E.B. Ashmore who formulated an early concept of defence against bombers which was essentially what Dowding and Park put into practice in 1940, with the additional help of radar. Ashmore's work was forgotten after the Armistice in 1919. A group called the Air Defence of Great Britain was set up in 1924 and Dowding became the Air Member for Supply and Research in 1931, but crucial work did not get underway till 1936.

Air Marshal Sir Kenneth Cross described how he joined his fighter squadron at Hawkinge in 1931. He described that before radar systems of mirrors were being tried to provide early warning of attack likely to be coming from France. Air Vice-Marshal Bird-Wilson compares the consequence of not having radar in the Battle for France with its existence in the Battle of Britain. Sir Kenneth Cross described how the original plotting of attacker's progress became increasingly sophisticated through the development of Dowding's and Park's plotting table. Air Marshal Sir Kenneth Parker, who was Chief Signals Officer at 11 Group during the Battle of Britain, spoke about how sector operations rooms on airfields were unprotected, being located sometimes in wooden sheds. Only following the devastating attack on Biggin Hill was this inherent weakness fully appreciated. Park appeared to panic about this, insisting the operation rooms in 11 Group be moved to temporary premises. He also insisted that the consequence of moving to inadequate premises would be disastrous. Parker was given permission by Park to create new operations centres, which involved moving to a school in Debden, a big house in Northolt, to an infant school at Hornchurch, and to a masonic hall in Southend. From a butcher's shop the operation room moved to a country club, while a big house was found for operations in Kenley. Dr Orange sums up the situation of the operations rooms: 'However battered it was, each part of the system stood the strain; it had the necessary flexibility.'

In December 1936 Park was selected to attend a course at 9 Buckingham Gate designed to promote greater links and inter- service cooperation. Those attending the course remembered Park shooting intelligent and perceptive questions at people such as Hugh Dowding and Clement Atlee brought in to speak to them. In July of the same year Park joined the embryonic Fighter Command that had been set up at Bentley Priory in Stanmore. In 1938 as Senior Staff Officer to Dowding he became second in command to Dowding with responsibility for fighting efficiency. In this period Park added to Dowding's confidence in him and the admiration of those about him for hard work, easily adopting the style for which he was to become known – flying to his command post ensuring he was fully appraised of what was happening within his organization. Now 46, Park was able to build on his twenty years' experience within the fighter element of the RAF.

Park won Dowding's support for his belief that tactical decisions could not be confined to the plotting table at Bentley Priory and that decentralisation was vital, a critical step. This is the period when Park forged the method by which Fighter Command would be capable of withstanding a long period of fighter operations. It was the time when the development of both the Hurricane and the Spitfire came to fruition. In 1938 Sholto Douglas, Assistant Chief of the Air Staff, was advocating the purchase of 450 Boulton Paul Defiants despite the fact that the aircraft was backward firing putting it at a disadvantage to contemporary German aircraft. Dowding and Park were in little doubt about its inferiority to both the Hurricane and Spitfire, and after agreeing to just two squadrons sought to put them in bases where they could do least damage.

The Munich Crisis in October of 1938 brought to a head the deficiencies in Fighter Command. There was a shortage of aircraft with only five regular squadrons and five auxiliary squadrons to meet the growing Nazi threat. Biplanes were still in service and there were large gaps in the nation's air defence coverage. As well as this there was a desperate need for support staff at bases and ground crew to service aircraft. There was an urgent need to build the infrastructure to support radio direction finding – radar. Park pondered the challenge of defence against fast flying aircraft and the formation that fighters should use in response to mass aircraft attack. He was aware that the guns presently mounted on existing fighter aircraft, .303 calibre, were inadequate to penetrate the shell of opposing fighter aircraft. By the beginning of 1939 Park was producing a manual of instruction for fighter commanders and outlining his belief that attacking enemy bombers would be protected by fighters.

Leslie Gossage, Commander of 11 Group before Park's appointment, as early as March 1939 raised the question of what should be the principal tasks and objectives of Fighter Command. Should the defending forces seek the large-scale destruction of the enemy or aim at the interception of bombers before bombing? In his reply Dowding spoke about the inherent dangers of seeking to match attacking aircraft on a one-to-one basis and how that made Allied airfields vulnerable to attack because no defence was available.

Dowding and Park were confronted with two major problems. In February 1940 the Commander of the French Fighter Group reported a repeated failure in his exercises to intercept incoming aircraft; the French lacked both an air-to-air system of communication and any form of radar. In a few months the inadequacy of the French Air Force would be glaringly revealed. Within the RAF itself Park and Dowding confronted reluctance from Bomber Command to fully cooperate in exercises that should have been taking place on a monthly basis. Park raised with the Commander of Bomber Command, Air Marshal Ludlow-Hewitt, his urgent need for cooperation with exercises testing the effectiveness of Fighter Command. This was crucial to the setting up of new radar installations and air warden warning provision throughout the country. It became clear that Ludlow-Hewitt had little concern for any cooperation outside his own Bomber Command. This also did little to advance ways of distinguishing between friendly and unfriendly aircraft.

On 20 June 1939 Park set the scenario for an exercise involving Bomber Command that would take place on 8 and 9 July. The attacking aircraft would come in east of Great Yarmouth approaching over the sea at around 2,000 feet. Park required that at least three bombers took part in each raid. At a conference on 24 August, Dowding sitting in judgement credited the rate of interceptions achieved as being 'reasonable'. However the lack of cooperation from Bomber Command was highlighted by the small number they made available for the exercise. A grim portent for the future came in a report from Trafford Leigh-Mallory, Commander of 12 Group, who ordered the evacuation of his operations room for ten minutes while the attack was in progress and his reaction to being caught by surprise by low flying aircraft was to mount standing patrols, which Park considered to be an overreaction.

The importance Dowding placed on Park's support is indicated by 11 Group, covering the crucial south-east of the country which Park commanded, being selected as the first to enjoy a General Post Office link to the new operations room. This distinction was not lost on Leigh-Mallory who nursed a grudge about not being selected to command 11 Group and being allocated 12 Group instead. Dowding's Group formations, including Park's 11 Group, highlighted the absence of real depth of thought on the consequences of total war on the country's civilian population involving attacks on shipping and other sources of supply. To the threat of submarine attack experienced in the First World War, attack from the air was not added. In relation to attacks on conurbations like London, Dowding correctly suggested in 1937 that hundreds of small fires as the result of systematic bombing would be beyond the control of any fire service.

Park had an operation for appendicitis on 8 March 1940 and on 13 April he learned of his appointment to the key group, number 11, as part of Dowding's planning. Park's group headquarters would be at Uxbridge. This had involved him in the purchase of a house close by which made the base easily accessible. Despite the intense pressure to create fighter defence during 1939 he had still found time to maintain his interest in sailing around the south coast with his family.

Park supported Dowding in his strong interest in radar. By August 1937 resources were found by Chamberlain, the new Prime Minister, enabling a chain of twenty stations to be established. These were to become the eyes of Fighter Command. The principal scientists involved were Robert Watson-Watt, who had described in 1932 radio waves bouncing off an aircraft and revealing information on its flight, and a Dr Appleton who had used cathode ray tubes to identify height. At one of the Group 11 stations, RAF Biggin Hill, Dr B.G. Dickens began research to use filtered radar signals to plot and convert the impulses into effective direction for interception. However, it was the station's commander, E.O. Grenfell, who established a working operations room model that Park was able to use in 1940.

In 1937 Neville Chamberlain had expressed doubts whether air parity with the Germans was affordable. It was decided to give priority to fighter defence, with the Hurricane being augmented by the Spitfire. Churchill recognised that scientific expertise in developments such as radar would also assist in providing world class air defence. In contrast, when war broke out, Hitler made the decision to place German radar advances in the hands of the German Navy and not use it for airborne detection.

As previously mentioned, Park was very much involved in simulated aerial attacks on Britain from 1938. It was apparent that a system of identifying friend from foe was needed. Radar in the turmoil of attack had its limitations, most strikingly the difficulty with identifying low-flying aircraft. This to some extent was overcome by the creation of the Observer Corps which Dowding and Park believed should work in conjunction with the new Radio Direction Finding Stations. The Corps was a more sophisticated observation unit than that set up in the First World War and designed to compensate for radar's shortcomings by enabling judgements to be made about the height of approaching enemy aircraft. It is important to note that they were only allowed to track aircraft already detected by radar stations.

Both Dowding and Park argued for retention of resources for UK Air Defence despite the demands of the British Expeditionary Force dispatched for the Continent when war broke out in September. As a further problem, the Air Fighting Committee and the Air Fighting Development Establishment, working to design tactics for air defence, had established the norm for fighter combat being flying in formation right up to July 1940. Park disagreed with this and placed responsibility on squadron leaders adapting to the realities of a fluid situation.

At the same time, the Germans had manoeuvred around restrictions by the Versailles Treaty to produce 2,000 aircraft supported by 20,000 officers and men. This was the daunting challenge for a Fighter Command taking its place alongside Bomber Command, Maintenance and Coastal Defence. The Dowding System was an air defence network which controlled both the flow of intelligence and the communication of orders during enemy raids. It included anti-aircraft guns, searchlights and barrage balloons. The country was divided into four geographical areas with the crucial 11 Group based at Uxbridge covering London and the south-east. 10 Group covering the south-west was under Air Vice-Marshal Quintin Brand. 12 Group covering the Midlands, East Anglia and parts of northern England was led by Leigh-Mallory. Northern England, the south of Scotland and Northern Ireland – 13 Group – was under the direction of Air Vice-Marshal Richard Saul. There was a further division at airfields referred to as sector divisions, each equipped

Scramble at a fighter base.

with operations rooms. What could not have been foreseen was that following the rapid collapse of France the main attack on Britain would come from captured airfields across the Channel making the south-east, Park's Group, especially vulnerable to attack and becoming the pivotal defensive force.

For the RAF the Munich Crisis in 1938 occurred at possibly the worst time. It followed frustrating unsuccessful exercises involving mock attacks on the east of England defended by Fighter Command working with Bomber Command acting as the attackers. These underlined to its commander, Ludlow-Hewitt, that he had inadequate resources at his disposal. By summer 1939, following further exercises, Fighter Command was able to demonstrate some of the defensive capability Dowding and Park were working on.

There were further problems. Dowding and Park faced a major challenge in seeking to wean traditionalists away from support for biplanes and achieve acceptance of the Hurricane and Spitfire. Aircraft such as the British Bulldog, supported by Air Vice-Marshal Sholto Douglas, denied the pilot a weapon and weighed half a ton more than the Hurricane. The '30s decade had opened with the financial consequences of the Great Depression and the air defence of Great Britain being lucky to escape with just a ten per cent cut in its budget. In 1933 when Hitler walked out of the League of Nations, the RAF fighter resource consisted of just thirteen squadrons of biplanes. At this

Kenley in 1938 – note the Gladiators still in use.

time prototypes of first the Hurricane and then the Spitfire at Woolston near Southampton were going on display at Hendon Air Show.

On 11 October 1938 during the Munich crisis Fighter Command's poverty in aircraft and manpower was sharply highlighted. Coupled with this was a shortage of aerodromes, a desperate need for ground crews to support aircraft movement, together with an absence of adequate staffing for guard duty security. Park's experience in the First War meant that he was immediately able to come to terms with these shortcomings on taking up his post at Uxbridge. He did not tolerate fools gladly, dismissing pilots who failed to recognise the key role that ground crews played in maintaining aircraft operation. Although there appears to have been a bias in favour of Bomber Command in the RAF, Fighter Command benefited from the lack of evidence that strategic bombing represented an effective response to enemy aggression. Chamberlain recognised that fighter defence was a cheaper option than building up Bomber Command as a deterrent to the growing strength of the Luftwaffe. During this time Churchill had become aware of Park's influential position in the planning of fighter defence in response to the huge displays of Luftwaffe capacity in Berlin.

Park's air defence responsibilities included the provision of searchlights around key areas to be defended. By the beginning of 1939 there were 135 squadrons in the RAF of which 74 were bombers, 27 fighters, 12 for army cooperation, 17 reconnaissance, 4 torpedo bombers and 1 communications squadron. During the early months of 1939 Park made himself available to visit elements of the Auxiliary Air Force and the Auxiliary Air Force Reserve. On 20 May he played an important part in organising displays at 60 air force stations and 18 other airfields that attracted a million visitors.

Only three days into the war, on 6 September 1939, 11 Group was involved in a serious incident related to friendly fire underlining how important it was to create a system clearly identifying fighter friends from foes. Radar reports showed incoming enemy planes and the controller of 11 Group sent 56 Squadron and 74 Squadron to intercept them. Unfortunately the Spitfires of 74 Squadron mistook the Hurricanes of 56 Squadron for enemy planes and shot down two of them. In bright sunlight they had dived on the Hurricanes killing one of the Hurricane pilots and forcing the other badly damaged into a crash landing. Keith Park was given responsibility for investigating what had happened. He had the three Spitfire pilots arrested and court martialled and instituted a toughening up of procedures to prevent a similar incident.

Sometimes it is the character of a place and a building that designates what emerges from its walls. As far as the Uxbridge Control Centre for 11 Group was concerned this certainly was the case. After being used in the First World War for a range of purposes it was formally adopted by the newly constituted RAF in 1918. In 1939 Keith Park watched with concern as the basement for the Operations Centre was finally created, despite subsidence from London clay, only being completed ten days before the outbreak of war. The Operations Room was developed from a series of rooms on two levels 60 feet underground reached by 76 steps. There was a large map table and squadron display boards featuring balloon and weather statistics. It was all part of the Dowding system linking Barrage Balloon Command, the Observation Corps, the radar chain and intelligence sources. Park's house was only a few yards from the Control Centre bunker which was entered through a small door where intelligence messages from Bentley Priory, Dowding's headquarters, were being received. From Uxbridge messages were sent to air force units allocating resources to meet German attacks. Men returning from Dunkirk were being processed after their return to Britain in the Uxbridge complex. On 26 July 1940 Uxbridge was attacked with a delayed action bomb and on 6 October by a single Junkers Ju88 bomber.

On 16 August 1940, when Churchill made one of several visits, Park was possibly the first to hear his ideas for his speech which personified the Battle of Britain: 'Never in the field of human conflict has so much been owed by so many to so few.' (Ismay suggests that this was developed in the car after the visit.)

On 6 and 15 September, the King, the Queen and Churchill were present at Uxbridge. Now known as Battle of Britain Day, 15 September is recognised as a day of crisis for Park in the campaign. On that occasion Churchill, transfixed by the drama of the occasion asked if there were any reserves. Park replied, 'There are none.'

11 Group had 7 sector stations: Kenley, North Weald, Debden, Biggin Hill, Tangmere, Hornchurch and Northolt. Uxbridge's bunker became the prototype for ones developed for 9 Group at Burton Hill, 10 Group RAF Box, 12 Group RAF Watnall, 13 Group RAF Newcastle and 14 Group Raigmore.

Park was not immediately taken with the role that women would play as part of the Women's Auxiliary Air Force (WAAF) who operated the plotting tables at Uxbridge. He initially expressed impatience with moves to increase women's roles within 11 Group but seems to have come to terms with a role for women as the war progressed.

Joan Fanshawe, one of ten special duty WAAFs, talks about the important contribution they made to the success of 11 Group's campaign. Their role was to provide Park with pin-point accuracy using blocks and arrows to indicate where the Luftwaffe were tracking. 'When the weather was good we were frantically busy because the planes were coming our way and we were getting our planes up from the airfield so the table was crammed with blocks and arrows,' she remembers.

Within Fighter Command there was argument about the location of operational airfields. Leigh-Mallory believed that 12 Group, covering the Midlands area north of London, should have twenty-nine of the available fighter squadrons. There were questions about in which Group airfields like Duxford and Debden should be located. In September Dowding issued an instruction drafted by Park to all group commanders that they should not go their separate ways but should give priority to good strategic practice.

Park was keenly aware of the low rate of production within the aircraft industry, only managing two Hurricanes and two Spitfires a day. This was to improve to six a day during the first months of 1940, helped by Park's developing relationship with Lord Beaverbrook who had been placed in charge of aircraft production by Churchill.

Sir Samuel Hoare, Secretary of State for Air, had recognised that the total level of British aircraft production of 2,550 was inadequate; it was clear that to meet the growing need of Fighter Command for Spitfires and Hurricanes, development of further new aircraft might have to be sacrificed. Dowding and Park had argued that fighter defence was more important than the manufacture of bombers. Bombers could be manufactured at a steady pace, but for the defence of Britain increased manufacture of fighter aircraft using firms like Fairey Aviation was vital. Meanwhile Beaverbrook was exerting his influence on both sides of the Atlantic to further increase aircraft production in Britain. An approach to Henry Ford for him to build Rolls Royce engines in America failed: 'You have enough motor manufacturers yourselves to make your engines,' Ford snapped back. In Beaverbrook, Dowding and Park had excellent support for their view that fighter production should take priority. Another aspect involving preparation for defence which coincided with Park's view of the comprehensive nature of fighter support was maintenance and repair and the strengthening of the Civilian Repair Organization or CRO. Methods had to be developed for the storage of spare parts and the repair of damaged aircraft. Low loading vehicles were developed to take damaged aircraft back to repair centres.

From July 1938 Park, when he had moved to Bentley Priory as a Senior Staff Officer, had effectively been second in charge to Dowding. At the age of 46 the appointment came at a optimal time in Park's life. His appointment to Fighter Command had been a fluke because originally the appointment had been given to Arthur Harris, but Harris had a preference for an appointment to a post in Palestine that had been given to Park, so the appointments were swapped. One immediate task was to develop a system of plotting tables so that a clear picture of not only the position of enemy aircraft could be displayed but also the availability of the fighter force to oppose them.

As mentioned, Park took on the task to develop a Manual of Air Tactics for a new conflict environment based on the new Hurricanes and Spitfires now coming into service. Unfortunately senior officers like Sholto Douglas and Donald Stevenson were still thinking of aerial combat in First World War terms. Park looking ahead said, 'In home defence work tactics do not interest the leader of a formation until he has been brought in sight of his target by the ground organization. There is the possibility of bombers having fighter escorts even in attacks on London.' He placed emphasis on flight leaders' initiative and eschewed any system dominated by drills but placed emphasis on an effective interaction within squadrons. What happened in practice in the peacetime training in which Fighter Command was currently involved tended to place safety above aggression in an attack situation against incoming enemy.

With the deployment of the RAF to France in support of the British Expeditionary Force the failure of tactics for the interception of the Luftwaffe became very apparent. General Harcourt commanding the fighter units in France summed this up: 'An attacking force which dashes into battle without a coordinated plan and proper control would be ineffective.' In all of this the need for the development of radio communication between aircraft and controllers on the ground was highlighted. Before moving to Uxbridge, Park promoted the integration of scientists into the team at Bentley Priory working on how the number of approaching aircraft could be effectively countered.

Park and Dowding had to invent the first operational defence system in the world. Their work on this started in 1936, but pioneering research dated back to the late 1920s and the work of Major General E.B. Ashmore, the founder of the Royal Observer Corps. There was willingness to engage with scientists working on radio direction finding and seeing how their work could be given practical application. By 1935 progress had been made and a research station set up, and by July 1940 systems were in place together with the Observer Corps, a Balloon Command and comprehensive air raid warning systems. The challenge was to develop systems where the information received could be analysed and plotted into vectors determining

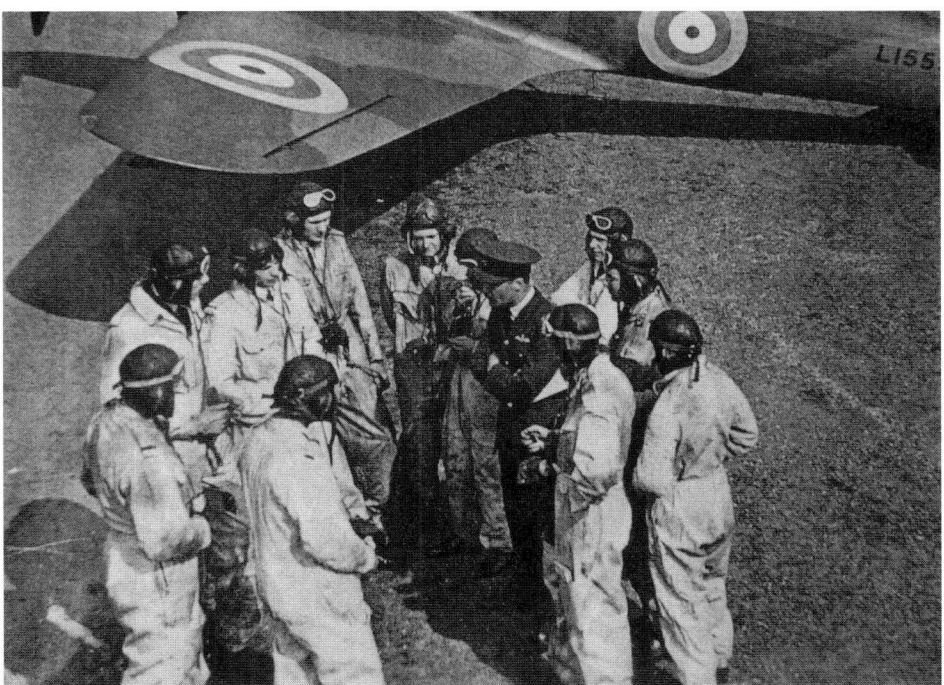

Delivery of first operational Spitfires in 1938.

height. There were questions about the vulnerability of radar stations like Ventnor and Rye dotted around the coast. A startling oversight was the failure to develop a coordinated way of picking up pilots who were forced down in the Channel during the first phase of the Battle of Britain when the Luftwaffe were attacking convoys. In contrast the Germans employed seaplanes for this purpose from the beginning of their attacks on Britain.

Some commentators have asked why RAF bombers singularly failed to effectively attack Luftwaffe aircraft on the ground preparing to attack Britain after Dunkirk. It was not until 1942 that British bombers showed a capability to overcome German defence of their airfields. As a consequence defence of the UK rested on Fighter Command because ideas of a counter-offensive against Luftwaffe airfields proved impractical.

Chapter 6

Dramatis Personae 1940

Marshal of the Royal Air Force Lord Trenchard: Park's close association with Dowding meant that his career would be determined by Dowding's relationships with the key figures in the Air Ministry. There was a long history of disagreements between Trenchard and Dowding going back to the First World War. Even though retired he was still able to exercise influence within the Air Ministry.

Air Chief Marshal Sir Cyril Newall: Won a high reputation in the First World War working closely with Trenchard. Between the wars he was Director of Personnel at the Air Ministry and deputy director of a school of air training. By 1926 he was Director of Operations and Intelligence and served in Cairo as the Commander of the Middle East. Crucially, in 1935 he took up appointment as the Air Member for Supply and Organization and was in a pivotal position for the RAF's development programmes leading up to the Second War. In 1937 he was appointed Chief of Staff and guided through the government's major expansion in the RAF.

Marshal of the Royal Air Force Sir John Salmond: Salmond was an aggressive man of action. He was closely linked to Trenchard in his disputes with Dowding during the 1930s. Crucially when an important committee was set up to examine the development of night fighters in 1940 he ensured Dowding was excluded from membership.

Sir Archibald Sinclair, Secretary of State for Air: Sinclair had close contact with Churchill and Sholto Douglas and appears to have played a key role in moves to sack Dowding and Park.

Air Marshal Sir Charles (Peter) Portal: Air Member for Personnel on the Air Council from 1939, promoted to acting Air Marshal on 3 September

1939. He became Commander in Chief of Bomber Command in April 1940. Later Chief of the Air Staff.

Air Marshal Sir Leslie Gossage: Played an important role in relation to Park's career as the Air Member for Personnel.

Air Chief Marshal Wilfrid Freeman: Responsible for the ordering of both the Spitfire and the Hurricane in the mid-1930s and organising increased production of them.

How Ready Were They?

At the Air Ministry as Air Member for Supply and Research, Dowding had been responsible for the newly developed Hurricane and Spitfire being integrated into the RAF. However, Watson-Watt, the developer of radar, places Dowding well below Douglas, Freeman and Newall in the support he received. In fact Park confirmed to the historian Denis Richards that Dowding required a great deal of persuasion before agreeing to support the introduction of radar. Even when the radar chain had been set up, Dowding was still ordering standing patrols until Park had connected radar stations to the headquarters in an exercise and showed how effective it was.

As if the organization of the defence of the country was not difficult enough, Park had to operate in an intensely political environment. From June to November, as events unfolded for the Battle of Britain, so too did the environment he operated in become more toxic. To achieve a full understanding of the personalities involved it is important to provide a background to who they were.

From the crucial stages of the Battle for France, Archibald Sinclair was Secretary of State for Air. Cyril Newall had been appointed Chief of the Air Staff in 1937 and he was to be in post through the Battle of Britain till he was replaced by Peter Portal. Stanley Bruce, the Australian High Commissioner, raised serious questions about whether Portal was up to the job. However, Bruce also criticized Dowding because of his focus on Fighter Command at the expense of Bomber Command. When the issue of who should replace Dowding arose it was Sholto Douglas's name which came to the fore. Park was to discover to his cost that Sholto Douglas was in close alliance with Trafford Leigh-Mallory, who had always believed that leadership of 11 Group belonged to him. Both Sinclair and Harold Balfour, the Secretary of State for Air, had travelled to Duxford to gather the critical opinions of Douglas Bader. There was no effort made to discover what other pilots felt in 11 Group. This agitation against Park and Dowding spread to the House of Commons and reached Churchill's ears. As the Battle continued into September and October a conspiracy developed aimed at sacking both Park and Dowding.

It is necessary to appraise the character of Leigh-Mallory, who was conspiring to replace Park. Dr Orange, Park's earlier biographer, says that if Leigh-Mallory walked past wearing a white coat he could easily be mistaken for a house painter. On the other hand, he might be taken for a brain surgeon. How can the qualities required for Fighter Command leadership be defined? They are not likely to be physical appearance; they may also not be simply wisdom or practical knowledge. They may be something more intangible. A German intelligence officer's appraisal had Park as 'defender of London' whereas Leigh-Mallory was relegated to 'the flying sergeant'. Park brought with him sound professional

Above left: Watson-Watt, inventor of radar, a vital part of Park's defensive strategy.

Above right: Air Marshal Dowding with whom Park formed a key relationship.

Volunteer trainee airmen in the late 1930s at their training camp.

Keith Park in dress uniform in the 1930s.

knowledge dating back to August 1926 from when he had studied air defence systems, producing a paper in 1926/7 based on his research. Park maintained that Fighter Command had existed before it was formally brought into being in 1936. He suggested it was nonsense to suggest that it could have been brought into existence without the basis of research and development which preceded it.

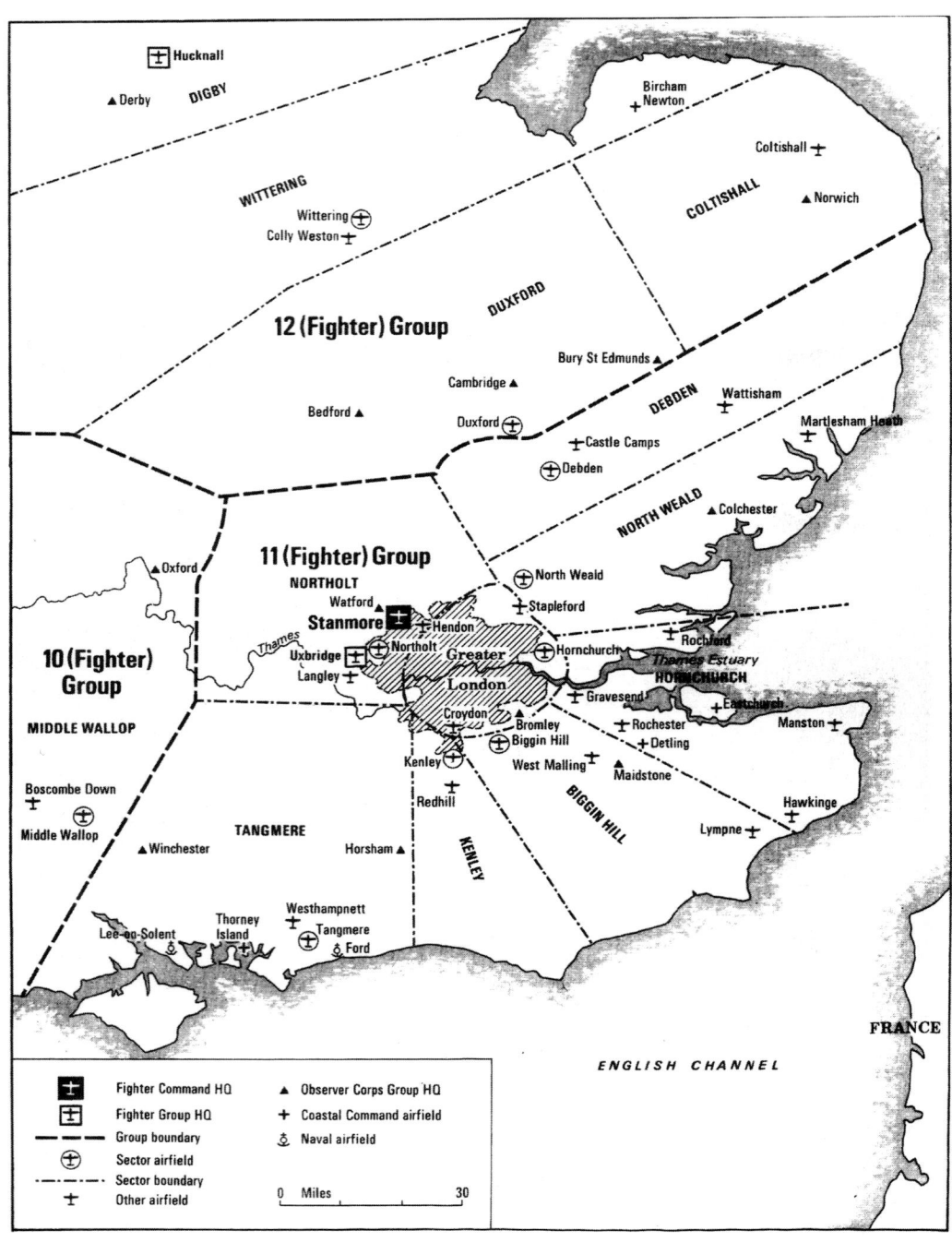

11 Group and the boundaries with 12 and 10 Groups.

Plotting table in the Operations Room.

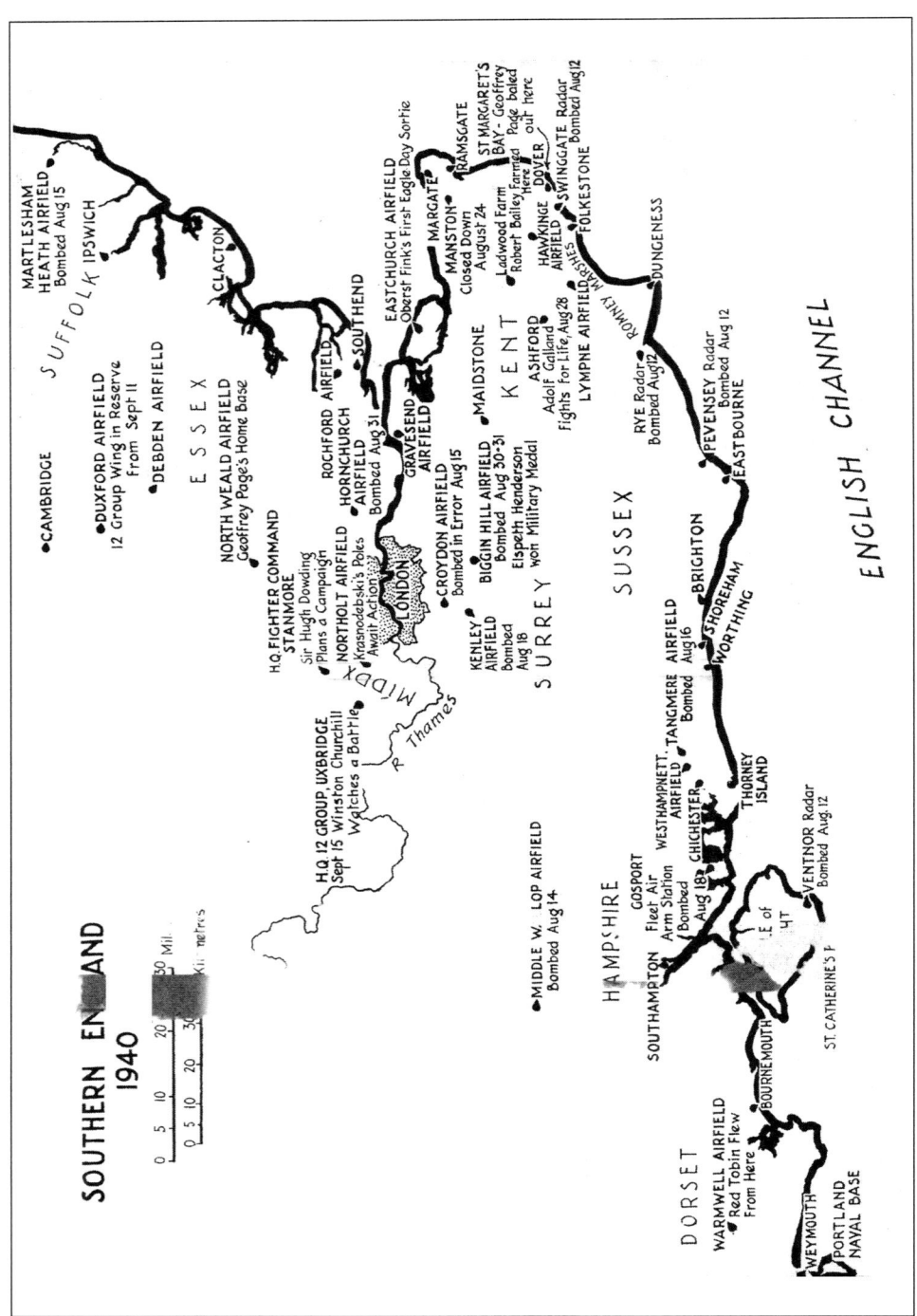

Fighter Command bases South of England 11 July 1940.

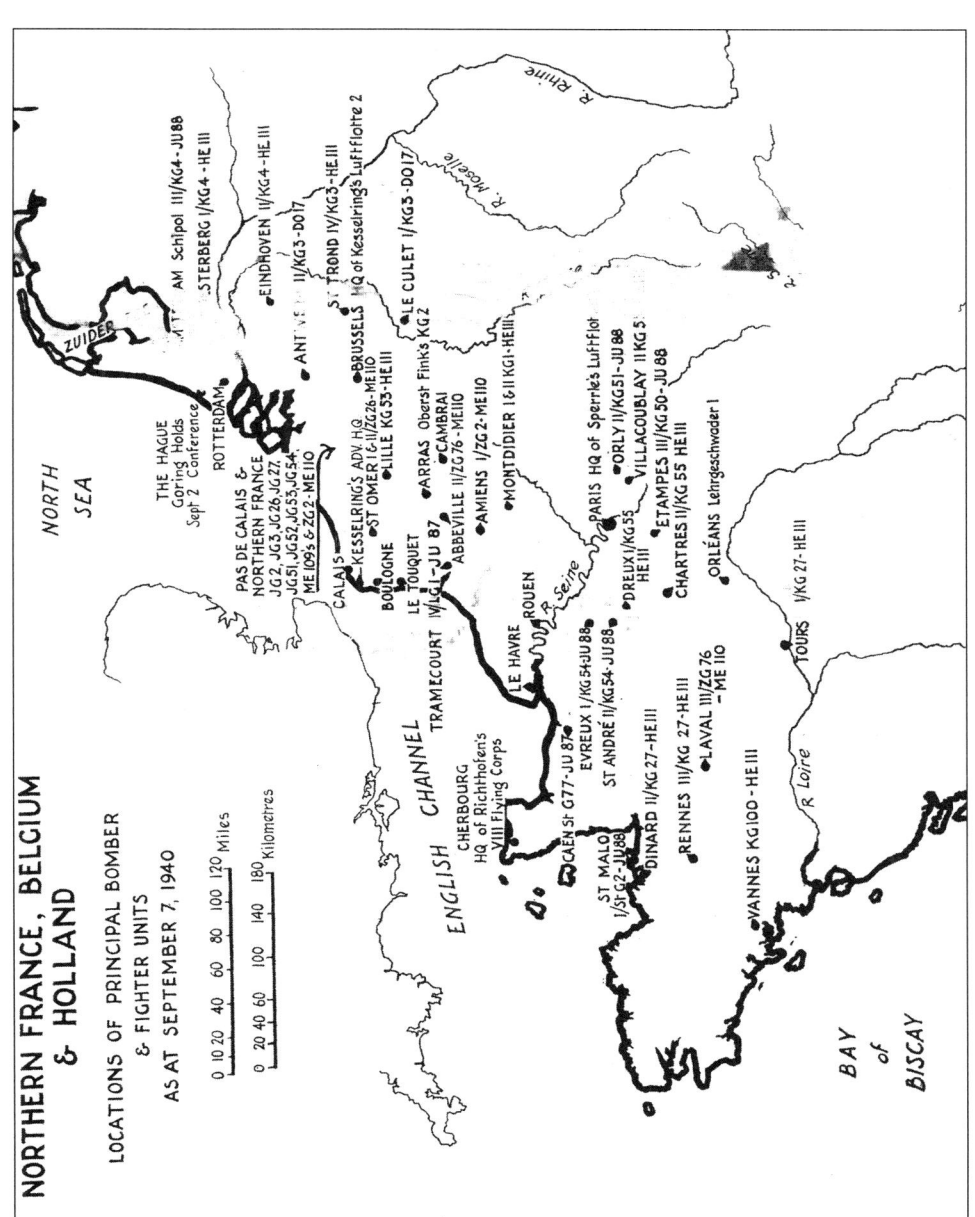

German bomber and fighter units in France

Park in his Hurricane

Chapter 7

Let Battle Commence

The air component of the British Expeditionary Force consisted of six squadrons, mainly Hurricanes and Gladiators. There were liaison difficulties with the French from the beginning with the airfield allocated to the RAF not being within the area allocated to the British army. This created difficulty for the supply of essential materials for the squadrons involved. Further it was found that the runways consisted of a type of clover which turned soggy in wet weather. There was also no support for the aircraft based in the hangers supplied by the French. When the major attack occurred on 10 May the Germans went around the Maginot Line, employing 86 Bf109s, 360 Bf110s, 300 dive bombers, 360 long range reconnaissance planes, 340 short range reconnaissance planes and 472 Ju52 transports. There was a whole series of disasters involving obsolete British aircraft, watched with horror by Fighter Command. On 7 May, twelve Blenheims were lost on an unsuccessful bombing raid, and a similar fate awaited more Blenheims when they were sent for sacrificial slaughter at Maastricht. On the other hand, despite the disasters the army was experiencing, pilots of Fighter Command were achieving good results in aerial combat involving Hurricanes despite the fact they were up against German pilots whose combat skills had been honed in the Spanish Civil War. The hard lessons from the battle for France for Park and Dowding were: the need for harmonised guns operating at 250 yards not 400; and to discard flying in tight V formation in favour of operating in pairs like the Germans which provided greater flexibility and allowed pilots to adjust to the reality of the situation they faced in conflict. Park and Dowding, working together, faced the reality that many planes and pilots had been lost during the Battle for France; but they benefitted from superior intelligence having unique access to information from Enigma, German failures in the provision of intelligence and German over-confidence based on success in Poland, Holland and Belgium.

Although the Luftwaffe's progress in the Battle for France was not a cake walk – Belgian air defence for instance destroying a large number of German aircraft – it was apparent that only Hurricanes and Spitfires represented any real opposition to it. When the war commenced Britain faced a Luftwaffe in possession of 4,161 aircraft: 604 reconnaissance, 1,179 fighters, 1,180 bombers, 366 dive bombers, 40 ground attack, 240 coastal, and 552 transports. By the beginning of April 1940 the numbers had increased to 5,178 with fighters increasing to 1,620, bombers 1,726, and dive bombers 419. Dowding and Park realised the challenge that faced them as the Luftwaffe moved to take possession of airfields on the Channel coast. Although German aircraft would be operating within the constraints of fuel supply, giving them only a short time over South East England, the proximity of these airfields gave the Luftwaffe a strategic advantage.

An Advanced Air Striking Force (AASF) was created on 24 August 1939 supported by a small fighter group unit when it moved to France on the outbreak of war. From the beginning there were difficulties in effective liaison with the French Air Force. As well as this the tactics deployed were inept. Even during the period of the phoney war up to the German attack on the Low Countries on 10 May 1940 it was becoming obvious through small exchanges that large fleets of planes like the Fairey Battles would not be an effect counter to Luftwaffe attack. Figures for losses from the opening days of the Battle for France speak for themselves: 10 May 40 per cent, 11 May 100 per cent, 12 May 63 per cent. On 10 May alone, the AASF lost 119 crews and 100 aircraft. Watching these events Park and Dowding observed how only the Hurricanes sent to France and a small number of Spitfires had been able to effectively defend the airfields used by the AASF. On 14 June the remaining Fairey Battles were returned to Britain and on 18 June Hurricanes and Spitfires returned. The RAF's losses in France had been around 1,000 planes, the French 1,400, as well as a total of 300 Dutch and Belgian planes. Total German losses were 1,800.

To Park and Dowding the intelligence they received indicated that in the very near future the defence of Britain itself was going to become paramount. On 15 May Dowding wrote to Park about how effectively he had pleaded in Cabinet about the dispatch of more Hurricanes and Spitfires to France: 'We had a notable victory on the home front this morning and the orders to send more Hurricanes were cancelled. Appeals for help will doubtlessly be renewed arriving with increasing insistence and I do not know how long this morning's work will stand. I will never relax my efforts to prevent the dissipation of the Home Fighter Force.'

Park, even on his sickbed suffering from appendicitis, was only too aware at the beginning of 1940 of the whole air defence picture. Although on 1 February eighteen new squadrons had been established, only two were fully equipped. Fighter Command was now to include coastal defence and anti-aircraft artillery plus searchlights. But in all this there was a lack of coordination, made very plain by the navy shooting down of two RAF planes above Boulogne.

The disintegration of the Allied armies had become apparent by 26 May 1940 and heralded the beginning of Operation Dynamo to evacuate troops on the beaches around Dunkirk. Park, operating out of Hawkinge airfield, had only 200 aircraft at his disposal spread over sixteen squadrons to provide air cover of the town and its beaches. He would have to ration his aircraft into morning and afternoon flights allowing a return of two patrols for rearming and re-equipping. On 27 May twenty-three German aircraft were shot down with the loss of sixty-four German aircrew. Major Werner Kreipe of 111/ KG2 reported: 'The enemy fighters pounced on our tightly knit formations with the fury of maniacs.'

By 28 May there were twelve patrols involving an average of two squadrons flying 321 sorties, confronting and being outnumbered by large formations of German bombers. Park could see the necessity to increase the number of planes in these patrols, but only at the cost of giving up on continuous coverage. This decision has promoted the view of soldiers trapped on the beaches being dive-bombed by Stukas that they had been deserted by the RAF. After the evacuation Vice-Admiral Lane leading the evacuation complained about the lack of support from the RAF. In fact air defence was taking place away from Dunkirk. By 29 May Dowding had approved Park having a free hand to increase the operating squadrons to four at any one time. Out of five Luftwaffe attacks Park was able to achieve three interceptions. The two missed ones were able to reach Dunkirk unopposed.

Park was able to observe the battle himself through regular flights in his Hurricane over Dunkirk. Bad weather from 30 May to 4 June reduced engagements but the consequence of fighter activity is shown by the fact that of 109 missions only 27 were up to full strength. The resultant German bombing and strafing led to evacuation being restricted to after dusk and early morning.

Continuous air cover demanded by the Admiralty was beyond Park's capability bearing in mind the resources at his disposal. He and Dowding were not prepared to commit aircraft from bases in the Midlands and northern bases to defensive operations which might be ultimately futile. Park and Dowding's 'fighter boys' flew up to the limits of their endurance and as the statistics reveal took a considerable toll of German aircraft.

Park had been able to unleash aces like Sailor Malan and Robert Stanford Tuck who claimed large tallies in the skies above Dunkirk and who would become household names. Far from failing the army and navy, RAF fighters had been able to prevent the Germans attacking at Dunkirk on two and half days of the nine-day evacuation.

We can picture Park in his Uxbridge headquarters controlling seven sectors and twenty-three squadrons. It was the world's first integrated air defence system. His operations room had been completed in 1939 and was similar to Dowding's at Bentley Priory although his large board only showed activity in his group. From the beginning of the Luftwaffe's attacks Park showed a mastery of the speed needed to respond effectively to changes in the Luftwaffe's plans of action. It was left to the commanders of his sectors to analyse what were feints by German aircraft and what represented a genuine attack. As well as his key sector stations, Biggin Hill, Debden, Hornchurch, Kenley, Northolt, North Weald and Tangmere Park, he had built up a series of satellite airfields for dispersal if his main airfields were under attack. There was some puzzlement why Hawkinge near Dover was not included as a sector station, being a training centre when war broke out on 3 September 1939.

Hurricanes arrived at Hawkinge on 19 September when No 3 Squadron flew in, and the following month 500 Squadron consisting of Blenheims arrived. It was one of the listening posts. 79 and 245 Squadrons were based there until the end of the Battle of Britain and almost a third of 11 Group spent at least a couple of days there while their airfield was experiencing enemy bombing.

From Uxbridge, Park had to decide how many aircraft from his precious limited resource he should scramble and where to scramble them. Information was displayed necessary for the decisions he was making, such as the location of both friendly and enemy aircraft represented as numbered blocks on the plotting table. A series of lights 'at standby', 'enemy sighted', 'ordered to land' were displayed on a tote board. Coloured discs were used to denote the state of the weather for each of the Group's sector stations and time was registered through a coordinated system of clocks and coloured indicators.

Initially 11 Group, usually operating out of British airspace, was almost invariably outnumbered in their twelve aircraft units by the Luftwaffe who were operating with forty to fifty aircraft. Park increased numbers so that two or three squadrons could operate in conjunction with a rotating platform of leadership. In practice a dogfight usually developed with every squadron seeking its best advantage.

There was regular discussion between Park and Dowding about the quality of pilots joining 11 Group. 'I have pilots here that are still thinking they are turning left and right, they have no idea what port and starboard are. There are pilots who think that the radio is for idle chit chat, they have no radio knowledge at all. Fourteen to twenty hours and they are given their wings … it's ridiculous.' Dowding's reply: 'I know but we must be prepared, London could be attacked any time, and we must be ready. These boys are young, keen and they're trying, they're intelligent enough that after two sorties they will have all the experience they need.'

The truth is that fighter pilots are made, not born. One of the far-sighted ways to train them was the Commonwealth training scheme where arrangements were made to ensure that anybody wanting to be involved in flying as a pilot, navigator, or wireless operator could join a scheme covering Australia, New Zealand and Canada. The fact that New Zealand gave it huge support is shown by a country of less than two million people producing well over 130 pilots for Fighter Command. In Britain the RAF Volunteer Reserve and the Auxiliary Air Force along with the universities were offering training. Johnnie Johnson, one of the Battle of Britain's top aces, however complained that the Auxiliary Air Force was the preserve of the rich. When interviewed for the AAF he was denied entry because he disagreed with fox hunting.

On 19 May, Park's report on Fighter Command's performance at Dunkirk was very different from that written by the Army and Navy: 'Our fighter pilots obtained such an ascendancy over the German bombers that during the last phase of the operation on sighting even a small formation of our fighters German bombers jettisoned their bombs in the sea. On one occasion a fighter who had used up all his ammunition made a feint against a German aircraft which fled causing it to lose control and plunge into the sea. There was victory inside this deliverance which should be noted. It was gained by the RAF despite the difficulty of defending Dunkirk.'

Chapter 8

After Dunkirk the Defence of Britain

After the fall of Dunkirk, Churchill outlined Britain's defence strategy involving a vigilant watch on the enemy's ports through RAF reconnaissance, and that activity in these ports would result in attack and destruction. He saw the secondary tier of defence as constant patrolling of coastal waters by the RAF and the detection of preparations of any invasion force. The pausing of the Luftwaffe's activity provided an opportunity to strengthen Fighter Command with more planes arriving at airfields and more pilots to squadrons. By 1 July the number of squadrons available to Fighter Command had increased from 37 to 48 with 29 squadrons of Hurricanes and 19 of Spitfires. Park was only too aware that the losses over Dunkirk had not been made up, but through an increase in production this deficit was being remedied. He was to write after the Battle of Britain, 'I was worried daily from July to September by a chronic shortage of trained pilots and it was not until the battle was nearly lost that all staff at the Air Ministry assisted by allowing me to borrow pilots from other Groups in Fighter Command and from the Royal Navy. Incidentally in December 1940 when I was posted to Flying Training Command, I found that the Flying Training Command Schools were only working at two-thirds capacity and were following peacetime routines being quite unaware of the gross shortage of pilots in Fighter Command.'

Chapter 9

Overture to the Battle

Following the Germans' dramatic advance in the Battle for France and the rejection of Hitler's peace proposals, the Germans began attacks on shipping in the English Channel as the first stage for full-scale invasion of Britain – Operation Sea Lion. The German High Command recognised the need for air supremacy prior to invasion and the need for the Luftwaffe to destroy the RAF. Attacks began on convoys on 10 July. Park quickly recognised the impossibility of providing adequate protection for these convoys when from 4 July the Luftwaffe sank several British and neutral-states ships as well as downing a considerable number of fighters.

On 14 July the Luftwaffe sank the *Island Queen* and damaged other vessels in convoy CW5. It was obvious to Park that he needed reinforcement for 11 Group and in response 141 Squadron was transferred to Hawkinge air base from Turnhouse in Scotland. Unfortunately this squadron was equipped with Boulton Paul Defiant fighters, a two-man plane with a single engine and four machine guns. They were to prove of dubious benefit to Park in clashes with Bf109s over the Channel. At 12:15 on 19 July when 15 Ju87s and 15 Bf109s crossed the Straits of Dover only nine of the Defiants (Park discovered) were able to take off; four remained grounded. Despite a squadron of Hurricanes and Spitfires being scrambled for defence, two British destroyers, *Griffin* and *Beagle*, were hit by bombs and all German aircraft returned to their base unscathed.

As the Luftwaffe's raid was completed, the Defiants were spotted taking off from their base at Hawkinge. Since the Defiants' relative success over Dunkirk, the Germans had worked out how they might be outmanoeuvred. Park read with concern the diary description of what happened: 'The enemy aircraft dived from out of the sun on to the Defiants and made their attack dead astern, preventing the rear gunners from firing. The Bf109s then pulled out in steep turns but their greater superior speed and the fact

49

that our aircraft were pulling out on opposite turns prevented our gunners from firing.' After the initial dive many attacks were delivered from below. A German pilot in his diary describes the shooting down of the Defiants: 'We dive sharply. My commander attacks the closest aircraft. Then everything happens with the speed of lightning. I fire a short burst. The Tommy emits a white stream of leaking fuel. Then it slowly turns over the right wing and descends vertically. I turn around quickly only to see Oberleutnant Otto Kath and Leutnant Herbert Wehnelt finish off one enemy each. These too turn slowly over their vertical axis and then descend. I swing in behind the British on the far right and open fire from a distance of 20 metres. My tracer disappears into the fuselage and wings. I give only a short burst. The same thing is repeated again: first a white stream and then the plane turns over – I got him! By this time we had shot down 4 and still the British cling to their close formation and rely on rearward firepower.'

German diaries reveal that they could not believe their luck as the remaining three Defiants were organised in sections flying in columns trying desperately to reach the English coast. Pichon the Luftwaffe diarist records how they followed these fated planes across the Channel: 'Now we had to be careful with the ammunition. I selected a plane that flew to the far right. Meanwhile we had gone down from 3,000 to 1,000 metres. I blast away with all my guns but he doesn't fall. I fire with a large deflection while turning and see the tracers hit the fuselage and the wings. Finally he goes down. A yellowish white streak marks his descent, which ends in a frothy water fountain in the Channel not far from the English coast.'

Park and Dowding were able to read descriptions of the death throes of the Defiant from German intelligence as well as reports from 141 Squadron which noted four pilots killed or missing and six air gunners missing. Park was forced to make 141 Squadron non-operational. Only a single Bf109 had been shot down. He had to observe that the tactic of each aircraft acting as a cover for the one in front had been unsuccessful possibly because 141 Squadron lacked operational experience in flying this aircraft. Park could not avoid the conclusion that his remaining Defiants would not be able to make an effective contribution to his defence strategy.

On 20 July the Luftwaffe mounted further attacks on shipping in the Channel. Park was aware of the vulnerability of German reconnaissance aircraft following convoys such as CW7 and scrambled 54 and 603 Squadrons to attack them, resulting in the shooting down of two armed Luftwaffe reconnaissance aircraft. As the convoy moved up the Channel, Park used radar to employ 24 fighters from 4 squadrons to defend the convoy, effectively diving on attacking aircraft out of the sun. This engagement threw into sharp relief the vulnerability of the Stuka dive-bomber. Eight aircraft from 32 Squadron cut their way through the protecting Bf109s to effectively attack dive bombers below them resulting in four being disabled. At the same time the escorting Bf109s were engaged by eleven Hurricanes from 615 Squadron and nine from 610 Squadron. Despite this success, the loss of the destroyer *Brazen* and the freighter *Pulborough* in the convoy was a bitter blow.

Göring was having to come to terms with the reality that any attack on Britain would require an approach totally different from that employed in the victory in Europe. The term 'Eagle Attack' was coined by him to describe a grand attack on the RAF. Rather than using the Bf109 and Bf110 fighters for defence of Luftwaffe bombers, Göring postulated that they should fly ahead of his bombers seeking to draw RAF fighters into conflict. Well aware of this tactic, Park was to insist to his squadron leaders that they should ignore the German fighters and concentrate instead on attacking incoming bombers. Göring was aware that his tactic made his bombers vulnerable: 'Should the worst happen, the bombers have to rely on their formation flight and coordinated fire of their gunners,' he ordered. Historians have suggested that he was not present at the German bases long enough and thus was unable to monitor his directive effectively. Göring allowed just four days for the reaction to his plans from his staff unaware that Dowding and Park were conscious of what was being planned as a result of the German code being broken by Enigma.

By 20 July the Germans had assembled 2,194 aircraft, of which 248 were dive bombers, 725 Bf109s and 200 Bf110s. Still in the process of recovering from the deprivations of the Battle for France, the RAF were able to count on 532 aircraft that were operational, featured by 224 Spitfires and 308 Hurricanes. However, because of the Group system of Fighter Command areas devised by Dowding, only 300 of these aircraft were available to Park for the defence of Southern England (11 Group). The Germans enjoyed a superiority of more than six to one in the 11 Group theatre after operations at this stage.

For the British the Battle of Britain commenced on 10 July while for the Germans it started on the 24th. On 24 July the Germans achieved through a radar installation the detection of ships in the Channel in sufficient time to launch attacks within the range of their aircraft. Park had to come to terms with the loss of five of his aircraft while managing to bring down two Ju87 bombers and 2 Bf109s. He was having to report to Dowding about his inability to offer anything like comprehensive protection to convoys moving through the Channel. It was a reality hard to bear in the light of convoy losses. Park quickly became aware that any of his pilots forced to ditch in the sea faced an unlikely prospect of rescue while the Germans had a comprehensive rescue system that often picked up British pilots as well as their own. An indication of declining British defence in the area surrounding the Channel was the decision of the Navy to abandon Dover as an operating base in the event of German attack through Operation Sea Lion.

Park was forced to withdraw 52 and 54 Squadrons because of the loss of six pilots in three days which included those with the most recent experience. Through discussions with Al Deere, a fellow New Zealander, who was an outstanding fighter ace, Park was aware of the qualitative difference between squadrons. 54 Squadron recorded a good number of 'kills' while several squadrons with no victories were losing eight pilots in two days.

On 27 July convoy CW8 suffered more losses than CW7 before it. Eight of its transport vessels were sunk while another five limped back to Dover for repairs. Ju88s obliterated a destroyer flotilla sinking its leader *Codrington* and disabling the destroyer *Walpole* and the sloop *Sandhurst* which were docked in Dover. Further attacks by He111s along the east coast resulted in the sinking of the destroyer *Wren* and damage to the *Montrose*. On 28 July the freighter *Orlock Head* was sunk by German bombers in the North Sea. Park was aware that these German successes from 5,378 sorties in the Channel and the dropping of 1,474 bombs resulting in the sinking of forty-seven British merchant vessels during July including four destroyers was a significant German success.

However, when the aerial battle is analysed the situation appears somewhat different. At the end of July the RAF's losses amounted to 88 fighters and 72 bombers against Luftwaffe losses of 186 aircraft. German pilots following previous easy victories in Europe were now confronted with an opposition capable of matching them. As August approached, Park was in regular discussion with Beaverbrook about stepping up aircraft production to replace the aircraft that had been destroyed. In fact 496 aircraft were coming off the production line at a rate of production the Germans could not match. As far as pilots were concerned Park now had 1,400 pilots in August as compared with 1,200 in July. In qualitative terms however, the loss of experienced pilots was felt very badly, particularly eighty squadron leaders and flight lieutenants. Park was only too aware of the mathematics he had to work with: three Luftwaffe aircraft had to be shot down for every one he lost. Could the system Dowding and Park had created withstand a full German attack?

On 1 August Hitler extended the fight to the British mainland under Directive 17 following the build-up of fighter and bomber resources in northern France and Belgium as well as making good the losses sustained by the Germans in the Battle for France. However there was evidence that the infrastructure supporting the Luftwaffe in France was breaking down with only twenty of the railway wagons containing aviation fuel reaching Le Mans *Transportgruppe*. The intercept evidence Park received made him aware of the difficulties the Germans were experiencing and helped him frame his tactics to exploit the Luftwaffe's fuel problems.

There were indications that Hitler, Göring and the Luftwaffe High Command were distracted by events marking their victory in France with *Luftflotte* 2 and *Luftflotte* 3 (Air Fleets 2 and 3) only slowly being brought up to strength and with a small number of bombers attacking shipping in the Channel and laying mines. Not until 17 July were two air fleets ready for an attack on southern England. This consisted of 1,200 medium bombers, 280 dive bombers, 760 single seater fighters, 220 twin engine fighters, and 50 long-range and 90 short-range reconnaissance aircraft. Some aircraft were targeted towards the north of England to keep elements of Dowding's 12 Group from being redeployed to the pivotally strategic south of England.

Göring's dislike of the navy's Commander in Chief, Erich Raeder, prevented effective liaison between the German navy and the Luftwaffe who refused to accept calls from the navy for support. Not until 11 July was the formal order given to attack coastal shipping to Luftwaffe commanders Hugo Sperrle and Albert Kesselring. However, the relationship between the Royal Navy and Dowding and Park was not much better, with complaints about a breakdown in communication from Vice Admiral Horton being greeted with the response from Dowding and Park to put them in writing. Night attacks on coastal centres began with the objective of reducing morale but were generally poorly targeted.

In this period when twelve convoys were passing through the Channel every day, a third were being attacked. Park realised that because of the limited time available to order aircraft to scramble in response to an incoming attack, effective defence was very problematic. A further difficulty for his shore batteries was the danger of RAF planes being shot down, as the instruction they received was to fire at any aircraft coming into range. With a demand for 41,000 tons of coal every week, 20 to 30 vessels a day were sailing between the Thames and the Bristol Channel. In this period Park saw 71 of his pilots killed, 19 wounded and 4 missing with 115 fighters being destroyed and 42 damaged. Of these, 45 Spitfires were shot down, 20 severely damaged, 64 Hurricanes shot down and 12 severely damaged and 6 of the obsolete Defiants shot down. The bases most heavily engaged were Hornchurch and Hawkinge with 74 Squadron based at Hornchurch claiming the first German fighter shot down on 8 July.

On 7 August there was an attack on convoy CW9, the largest convoy so far in the war consisting of twenty cargo vessels. Attempts were made to slip through the narrowest part of the Channel in darkness but they were seen by German radar and three vessels were sunk by torpedo boats. The Luftwaffe attack from Luftflotte 2 involved Stukas and escorting fighters. Park's response was to commit three squadrons and although they managed to hold off the Stukas they lost four Spitfires in accounting for two Bf109s.

This engagement was followed by intelligence from the RAF station at Ventnor on the Isle of Wight that a formation of 57 Ju87 dive bombers and 30 Bf109s and Bf110s were approaching the convoy. In theory there was enough Luftwaffe fighter protection to allow the Stukas to gain access to the convoy, but in practice all the Ju 87s were shot down. However, of convoy CW9 and its twenty ships, only four vessels limped into Swanage Harbour.

From 10 July to 12 August, the first stage of the Battle of Britain, the focus of the Luftwaffe attacks was on Channel convoys and selected mainland targets. The Luftwaffe strategy was to try to lure Fighter Command into conflict with their numerically superior fighters. Dowding and Park refused to commit large numbers of squadrons to Channel protection. Through careful husbandry they were able to increase the number of aircraft they had available to 740. Because squadrons could not be scrambled fast enough to engage with enemy attacks there was no alternative but to have his squadrons on almost constant patrol. Dowding and Park had succeeded in keeping many of their Spitfires from service in France. Following the loss of Hurricane squadrons as a result of the Battle for France, they faced a real prospect of defeat as airfields were overrun and there was no infrastructure to support them. 'I saw my resources slipping away as a sacrifice. It was as if you dashed a glass full of water into a forest fire in the hope of putting it out for defence of Britain like sand in an hour glass,' Dowding commented. Of planes and aircraft in the Battle for France St Exupery, the French writer, said, 'Crew after crew being offered as sacrifice.'

In France there was a failure of the Wellington bombers to effectively connect with their fighter protection. Despite this 'Sailor Malan' and Bob

Stanford Tuck, RAF aces, were registering significant kills against the Luftwaffe.

On 5 June the Luftwaffe began reconnaissance raids over England. The RAF was facing a crisis because of loss of spares and essential material for aircraft support that had to be jettisoned in France. However due to Park's link with Beaverbrook, production of Hurricanes and Spitfires rose from 325 in May 1940 to 496 in July.

On 14 June Park was the leading speaker at a conference at Northolt air base called to discuss fighter tactics. How should squadrons operate – singly, in pairs or in larger groupings? This was the curtain raiser for the major debate about Big Wings. Also discussed was the methods that might be used to separate bombers from their accompanying fighter protection. Park with his mind going back to the First War ruled out more than two squadrons being billeted together with additional squadrons being moved to satellite airfields. Finally he emphasised that there was a fundamental purpose to attack the incoming German bombers and not to get into dogfights with their accompanying fighters.

Support for the war demanded an Emergency Powers Act to control the movement of labour into the aircraft industry and was paid for by a tax of 18 shillings in the pound partially at higher incomes. Park now had responsibility for a defensive ring around London focused on his 11 Group ranging from Northolt airfield to North Weald, Hornchurch in Essex, Biggin Hill in Kent, Kenley in Surrey, and Tangmere near the Sussex coast. It soon became apparent to Park there was an acute danger to his airfields with the Luftwaffe now beginning to operate from the Cherbourg Peninsula and St Omer. However, it became clear with information derived from Enigma that Hitler lacked an overall strategy for the invasion of Britain.

The *New York Times* reported the opening of the Battle of Britain: 'The gunfire rolled like thunder. One flight of raiders was split into two parts by anti-aircraft fire which kept some of the Luftwaffe performing aerial acrobatics while British pilots engaged the others.' By 19 July Park had learnt of the lack of manoeuvrability of his Defiant aircraft and the handicap of the planes' guns. He had to watch them literally falling from the sky in every conflict despite being moved from Hawkinge to West Malling away from conflict areas.

What profile is it possible to draw of Air Vice-Marshal Keith Park as he prepared to lead 11 Group into the Battle of Britain in the first weeks of July 1940? He has had twenty-five years' experience of working with fighter aircraft and has a profound knowledge of their operation. His experience with the RFC has marked him out to be a superb leader, extremely task orientated, ruthless, tough, with a no–nonsense attitude. Park possessed an excellent head for detail coupled with a rational, independent mind. His appointment brought to this key leadership position both physical and mental courage. He might be seen as austere and stern but this was coupled with a high level of personal integrity built upon his Christian faith. Some of those who worked with him considered him humourless with an ability to put some people's backs up. But against this was a considerable ability to put people at ease despite impatience with small talk. Park manifested great skills as a communicator.

Park's tactics as the expected attack became clear were to meet the greater strength of the Luftwaffe with pairs of squadrons and hopefully supplement his numbers from 12 Group to the north and 10 Group to the west. The attacks on fighters were to be avoided if possible with the bombers as the principal target. As the battle moved into its second and third phases the need to protect 11 Group airfields became clear as they became a prime Luftwaffe target. Bombers were to be destroyed, Park said, before they reached their targets, were in the act of bombing their targets, when they were returning to their base after bombing, had been detached from their fighter escort, or when they had exhausted their ammunition.

Lord Beaverbrook, with whom Park worked to maintain supply of Hurricanes and Spitfires.

Park with the Hurricane he used to visit 11 Group bases.

Luftwaffe commanders, Generalfeldmarschall Albert Kesselring and Generalfeldmarschall Robert Ritter von Greim.

Reichsmarschall Göring.

MONTHLY OUTPUT OF FIGHTER AIRCRAFT JUNE - OCTOBER 1940			
MONTH	PLANNED	ACTUAL	DIFFERENCE
JUNE	1.164	1,163	-1
JULY	1.061	1,110	+49
AUGUST	1,143	1,087	-56
SEPTEMBER	1,195	908	-287
OCTOBER	1,218	917	-301

The table below indicates the number of fighter aircraft available to squadrons for operations:

AIRCRAFT AVAILABLE FOR OPERATIONS		
MONTH	DAY	TOTAL AIRCRAFT AVAILABLE
JUNE	22	565
	29	587
JULY	6	644
	13	666
	20	658
	27	651
AUGUST	3	708
	10	749
	17	704
	24	758

Aircraft production figures.

Göring talking to Luftwaffe pilots before Eagle Day.

The plotting operations table at work, Uxbridge.

Chapter 10

The First Phase

Massed Luftwaffe bombers accompanied by Bf109 fighters at 20,000 feet represented the Germans' first response to fulfilling Göring's demand to crush the RAF. Park quickly realised that this effectively exposed the bombers to direct attack. He placed his fighter squadrons around Brighton and Portland Bill on standby with a warning to be vigilant in case of a direct attack on south coast airfields finding his aircraft still grounded. His instruction was 'Engage the enemy before he reaches his coastal objective.' The Spitfires were to target the Luftwaffe fighters while Hurricanes should seek to destroy German bombers, especially the Dorniers. As well as a loss of pilots in the Battle for France Park faced a severe shortage of competent formation pilots and section leaders. In practice in each squadron there were just two or three pilots with the skills and experience to mount effective attacks. 'During August,' said Park, 'our squadrons were suffering casualties at a rapid rate. At one stage our squadron strength was down to an average of 9 pilots. We were sent replacement pilots, young and straight from operational training units, and most had limited training on Hurricanes and Spitfires.'

Squadron Leader John Thompson, 111 Squadron: 'It was normal for us to give new pilots a form of simulated combat training, something they should have got in their training, but all they got there was how to fly the aircraft, combat training was left to us fellows at the operational squadron that they had been posted to. In most cases, especially when operations were at their height, there was no time for this, and many a time new pilots would arrive in the morning only to be thrown into combat at midday. Needless to say quite a few of them did not return from that first combat experience. It was sickening and disheartening and sometimes you get to wonder what chance these young recruits have of survival.'

As well as having poor intelligence, Göring and other Luftwaffe leaders failed to recognise the significance of the radar stations in the British radar chain that their reconnaissance aircraft crew were telling them about. Galland

and other junior commanders spoke of their puzzlement that the RAF always seemed to be present in significant numbers once an attack had been launched. Park knew that his greatest threat was to the sector stations within easy flying time for the Luftwaffe. If this was the case, very little time existed to scramble his aircraft to their defence. It is significant that both Galland and Mölders, Luftwaffe leaders, complained about the way that British fighters always seemed elusive and reluctant to be drawn into battle, reflecting Park's strategy to maintain reserves of fighter capacity. His concept of the battle just commencing was one of attrition and wearing down the Luftwaffe's reserves. On 1 June Park received four more squadrons made available to him which were flown from Wick to Tranmere. The limitations of radar were well known; in addition, Park knew that the Spitfire's Browning .303 machine guns were inferior to the two 7.9 mm machine guns possessed by the Bf109 German fighter. He recommended the replacement of the Hurricanes' and Spitfires' existing machine guns with guns with a larger bore and more rapid rate of fire. He was in regular conversation with 'Sailor' Malan, one of his squadron leaders and an air ace in his own right, about evolving tactics to the new realities of fighter combat over Britain. Lord Beaverbrook was stepping up aircraft production much to Park's relief: 'I was never grounded because of lack of aircraft,' Park was to say.

County of Chester Squadron awaiting call to scramble.

Ready for the scramble.

The operations room at Kenley 11 Group base.

Rescue of downed pilots from the Channel.

Refuelling and rearming.

Chapter 11

Park and the 'Few'

Both Park and Dowding had correctly read the runes as far as the rise of the Nazis from 1933 was concerned. German rearmament bolstered Fighter Command's advocacy for new aircraft, particularly the Spitfire and the Hurricane. However, there was a need for skilled pilots to fly the new planes. Park exploited his New Zealand contacts with the New Zealand High Commissioner, Bill Jordan, in London, who had led New Zealand's opposition to aggressive actions by Italy and Germany in the League of Nations. Both Jordan and the New Zealand Prime Minister, Peter Fraser, had been at odds with the British government's appeasement of Germany. Their advocacy helped Dowding and Park's pleas for increased spending on air defence. In practical terms, as war became a certainty, Fraser encouraged the training of New Zealand pilots, many of whom joined the RAF. Some of the names of these young New Zealanders joined the pantheon of air aces who Park met on a regular basis as he flew around the sector airfields in his Group. From them he gathered an up-to-date impression of the conflict. Some of these men, like Alan Deere and Colin Gray, enjoyed more than nine lives from Dunkirk through to the Battle of Britain.

On Park's recommendation, Gray had received a DFC from George VI after baling out over Dunkirk and managing to return to his base within nineteen hours. In no way daunted, Gray immediately recommenced duty. John Kent, or 'Kentski' as he was known, a Canadian, had been based at Uxbridge when it was just a depot. In 1937 he was one of the test pilots on the Spitfire working to improve its high-altitude performance. An American volunteer, Billy Fiske, joined Park's pilots at Tangmere. Polish and Czech refugee pilots who had arrived in Britain presented a problem: their lack of English disguised their considerable experience in the air. It was assumed that they were novices and the RAF insisted erroneously on them following a complete course of instruction.

Geoffrey Allard from 85 Squadron was killed in a crash near Debden and Group Captain Allan Wright DFC, a graduate of Cranwell in 1938, operated from

Tangmere until he was shot down by a Bf109 on 20 October 1940. Others, like Mike Crossley, Victor Beamish, Archie McKellar, Jim Hallowes, Jamie Jamieson, Hawke Eye Welles, Frank Carey, Gordon McGregor and Willie Knight, were watched over paternalistically by Park. Every death was a source of deep sorrow.

Park summarized the tactical issues he faced in the following way: 'The main problem was to know which was a diversionary attack and to hold sufficient squadrons in readiness to meet the main attack when they could be discerned from unreliable information received from radar stations sometimes after they had been bombed.' He began the battle with only three training units supplying new pilots and he was to discover the ones that existed were not operating at nearly full capacity to replace the deficit in pilots for 11 Group. The real advantage he possessed was being aware of genuine weaknesses in the Luftwaffe strategy for attack through significant intelligence breaking of German codes. He was conscious of the continuing tactical error of the Luftwaffe placing over-emphasis on attack – a legacy of over-optimism following victories in Poland and France.

In the Luftwaffe there were quarrels about where the fighter protection for bombers should be placed, with leaders like Galland complaining that if they were alongside the Luftwaffe bombers they would be sitting ducks for RAF fighters. He commented, 'We saw the advantages of our experience in the Spanish Civil War being thrown away. We had to travel straight and level with the slow-moving bomber stream and were forbidden to engage the British fighters unless we were attacked. This meant we were compelled to submit to the Spitfires and Hurricanes the advantages of height, speed and above all the fighting spirit and aggressive attitudes which work for all fighter squadrons.'

One of the features of German bombers was their design as flying artillery providing support for advancing ground units. The Ju87 and 88, the Do-17 and the He111 lacked the range, the bomb capacity and the defensive armament to accomplish what was demanded of them in the Battle of Britain. The Bf109 lacked armour and range to adequately defend German bombers, while the Bf110 lacked the speed and range requirements to defend itself adequately, let alone keep the bombers safe. The British possessed two excellent fighter aircraft in the Hawker Hurricane and the Supermarine Spitfire. The Germans, who had kept their advances in radar secret, could not imagine the British had been ahead of them in development. They had underestimated the effectiveness of the air defence system developed by Dowding and Park. German intelligence had seized on comments within the Air Ministry seeing Park as humourless and irascible.

Chapter 12

Rising to the challenge

How was Park able to survive in the opening weeks of the Battle of Britain with far fewer planes than the attacking Luftwaffe? It was achieved through a very careful husbanding of resources. He was supported by an integrated anti-aircraft provision attached to 2,286 guns linked to 4,128 searchlights. There were 112 Spitfires and 341 Hurricanes available for defence in July. However he had only 821 combat-ready pilots he could call on.

From the outset Park found it difficult to rely on Leigh-Mallory's 12 Group when his lack of planes and pilots reached a crisis point. This confirmed Park's opinion of Leigh-Mallory as an operational commander. Park expressed concern that Leigh-Mallory insisted on operating in an independent way ignoring criticism from Dowding. Dowding wrote to Leigh-Mallory taking up the charge made by Park: 'I have delegated tactical control to groups and sectors but I have not delegated strategic control and the threat to the line must be regarded as a whole and not parochially.' Leigh-Mallory did not appear to accept this instruction and wrote to the sectors in his group designating how they should operate. Dowding's letter reminded Leigh-Mallory of the vital role his sector at Duxford would play in the defence of London. Dowding asked if it should come within 11 Group; Park convinced him it should be in 12 Group. In retrospect the significance proved to be that if he had control of Duxford he would have been Douglas Bader's commanding officer, someone who turned out to be one of Park's sternest critics in the Big Wing controversy. It was pointed out to him that Dowding's strategic planning did not allow for more than three squadrons at one aerodrome and that a single squadron controller should not be expected to manage more than four squadrons. In contrast he found in Brand, the South African Air Vice-Marshal at 10 Group, someone always willing to lend support. Within the Air Ministry there was discussion whether the bases in the vulnerable South East should be abandoned because of the need for defending aircraft to climb above the attacking Luftwaffe from nearby France and Belgium. Park and Dowding disagreed with this defeatist view because a retreat such as this would send a message of capitulation to the Germans. Park's practical advice to his pilots was 'Attack the one in front. If you shoot them down the formation will break up in confusion. Then you can take your pick.' Dressed in his white overall suit Park travelled to his bases in his Hurricane OK1 making direct contact with all ranks in 11 Group. While generally the RAF was achieving a greater number of kills there were bad days, such as 19 July when losses were greater than those of the Luftwaffe. In addition, some limitations were coming to light between the Spitfire and the Bf109, which could execute tighter moves and was around 20 mph faster. In practice Park had less than ten minutes to scramble his planes. One of the solutions he employed was to take off from airfields like Hawkinge away from the incoming Luftwaffe enabling his aircraft to achieve the necessary height advantage.

Gaps in 11 Group quickly opened up with fifty-four pilot losses being recorded. The outdated V-formation tactics were quickly discarded. He was also finding that in practice the boundaries between groups drawn by his planning with Dowding and meant to be flexible were in practice too rigid between 11 and 12 Groups.

The first Luftwaffe attacks involved fighters flying high and offering no real protection to their bombers. There were attacks on coastal centres on the south coast such as Brighton and Portland Bill. Park and his squadron controllers needed rapid response to meet these attacks within the thirty minutes available to them; delay ran risks of aircraft being caught on the ground. From the outset the failure of the Germans to take out elements of the radar chain was crucial in Park's survival plans. He commented, 'Without signals the only thing I command is my desk at Uxbridge.' The first phase of the Battle consisted of attacks on shipping in the Channel, with bombing of 18 coal ships, 4 destroyers and frequent episodes of mine laying by the Luftwaffe. The cost of this to the Germans was 31 fighter planes in these spasmodic confrontations restricted largely to the south coast. On 16 July, Hitler issued a specific order to prepare for invasion and Göring promised him that he could destroy the RAF in four days. The strategy as far as it existed was to defeat the RAF, Britain's war industry and supply lines, achieve capitulation and occupy Great Britain.

Air Chief Marshal Dowding, whose retirement had been postponed and who was scheduled to retire in October 1940, was Göring's opponent. He said, 'Mine was a defensive role of trying to stop the possibility of invasion and then giving the country a breathing spell. It was Germany's objective to win the war by invasion and it was my job to prevent this invasion taking place.'

Early Luftwaffe attacks were nuisance raids with the London conurbation being scrupulously avoided from attack. Park observed that at first as far as Londoners were concerned the only reminders of these raids were anti-aircraft gun emplacements, barrage balloons and the occasional searchlight. The Germans were seeking to gauge the speed and efficiency of the RAF's response to these incursions. Park was fully aware of this and played his cards carefully by limiting his response to only where necessary as the Luftwaffe carried out light bombing of Portsmouth, Plymouth, Newcastle and Merseyside.

Park in discussion with his pilots.

Chapter 13

Touch and Go

Hitler's response to Bomber Command's raids on the Ruhr was to seek from Göring a brutal response as soon as the Luftwaffe had established themselves in their bases near the French Channel coast. Göring ordered commanders of Luftflotten 2, 3 and 5 to immediately set in train planning for major attacks on Britain. A decision was made to make 5 August *Adlertag*, Eagle Day, when mass aircraft attacks would take place hitting a geographical line from London to Gloucester. Park and Dowding had intelligence indicating that this would be achieved within four weeks through the employment of 1,300 aircraft.

On 8 August, Galland, one of the Luftwaffe's leading organisers of the strategy, outlined how they would approach destroying the RAF, and stated, 'Our method of attack this time will be in far greater numbers than before. We still did not want to engage in aerial combat over English soil because that would mean a shorter stay for actual combat and we had to make sure we had enough fuel to get back to bases. By engaging in combat in mid-Channel we were able to engage in dogfights for more than twice the time and not only was it a short distance back to base, but if we had to ditch, our rescue would be guaranteed. However if we attacked in large numbers the RAF would detect us and draw fighters from their bases in larger numbers. Our response to this would be to bring up a second wave that would give us an absolute advantage.'

Dowding and Park, having read this through intelligence sources, responded through Dowding's communiqué to Air Ministry officials on 11 August: 'The enemy is getting closer every day. To succeed in our task we must be there to confront them before they are in any position to inflict any damage. My pilots and our planes are our frontline of defence along with our normal defence systems which we must agree, must be improved and updated. In recent weeks my pilots have proved they can stop the advancement of the Luftwaffe but our radar although doing its best can do better. You have to understand that German aircraft formations approaching at 200 mph leave my pilots just 20 minutes to reach operational height and make an interception. With the time we have we are intercepting the enemy too late and too low. The way things are the Germans could bomb large areas of our cities and towns at any time they wish to.'

Historians argue over when the Battle of Britain actually started and indeed the dates of the various phases. Officially 10 July is recorded with the first phase lasting until 12 August. I am taking 8 August as my starting day and this leads into Phase 2 of the official record starting on 13 August. On 11 August, Park, gifted with an almost intuitive ability to guess where the Luftwaffe would attack, realised that an attack on Dover presaged a major attack coming out of the airfields on the Cherbourg Peninsula. He was forced to scramble Hurricanes from Hawkinge and Spitfires at Manston and Kenley. The Luftwaffe attack consisted of 56 Ju88 heavy bombers, 67 Bf110s and 30 Bf109s. It should be noted that German historians believe the Battle of Britain continued till the war ended in 1945. A distinctive aspect of phase 2 was the failure of Luftwaffe attacks to neutralise the British radar system despite all-out attacks featured in Eagle Day on 13 August. What became clear about Göring's strategy was that it operated on the false premise that all the country's fighter reserves were based in the south of the country. Despite this, thirty-four of Park's fighters were destroyed on the ground on this day.

At 9.45 on 11 August Ventnor spotted a large German raid approaching. Park and Brand from 10 and 11 Groups agreed a joint response would be necessary bearing in mind the direction it was approaching. The focus of the German attack was against the naval bases at Weymouth and Portland. The RAF claimed 32 victories at a cost of 16 fighters and 10 damaged aircraft. The death toll of Fighter Command was fifteen with a number being wounded. 10 Group lost a sixth of its serviceable fighters. A more realistic analysis shows that fighting between 8 August and 11 August resulted in the loss of 74 German planes and 52 British fighters.

On 12 August Park heard reports of a large formation of Junkers bombers approaching Portsmouth. The fifty barrage balloons above the city were ineffective. In fifteen minutes the docks, warehouses, railway station, oil tanks, fuel tanks and berthed ships were all hit by bombs. This level of devastation was achieved despite anti-aircraft fire from land as well as vessels in the harbour. Park noted that the German bombers were becoming more adroit at fending off attacking British fighters. Thirteen British aircraft were shot down and four damaged on this day and eight RAF pilots were killed. Reliable analysis has German losses at thirteen, the same as Fighter Command.

Damage to 11 Group airfields would become a major concern. As early as 1938 Park and Dowding had anticipated this happening and had

New Zealand air ace Al Deere.

created blast-proof pens for their aircraft at Manston. Alan Deere wrote: '54 Squadron landed at Manston later in the afternoon, after the second engagement, to be met by a very shaken body of airmen and a no less shaken gathering of 600 Squadron pilots. The airfield was a shambles of gutted hangers and smouldering dispersal buildings all of which were immersed in a thin film of white chalk dust which drifted across the airfield and settled on men, buildings and parked aircraft with the manner and appearance of a light snow storm.'

Reading reports of gutted air bases could give the impression that a one-sided battle was taking place but in reality it was far from that. Pilot Officer Gray, one of the large group of pilots from New Zealand, provides another perspective. Gray, from the suburb of Papanui in Christchurch had arrived in Britain on the *Rangitata* in the last days of 1939. He joined 54 Squadron and became an acting pilot officer at Hornchurch despite almost writing off his aircraft on an initial flight in the presence of Dowding. In this crucial period in mid-August he proved himself one of the outstanding pilots of Fighter Command. On 12 August, Manston was bombed by Bf109s and Bf110s. At 25,000 feet Gray shot down one of the enemy and fatally damaged another, following it right to the French coast. On 13 August several attacks on airfields took place and on 15 August there was fighting over Dover and Dungeness. In all Gray was credited with four victories and four probables in this period of a few days.

Huge credit must be given to the ground crews working at 11 Group airfields around the clock, patching, repairing and replenishing the battle-scarred Hurricanes and Spitfires taking part in the dogfights above them. Meals and sleep had to be taken when any respite occurred. For pilots and ground staff alike there was the constant demand to come to terms with the deaths of the many who were killed. When Hornchurch was bombed Gray moved to Biggin Hill from where he was moved away to Catterick along with just five who survived from his squadron. Of the 11,000 Kiwis who served in the RAF between 1939 and 1945, 3,200 lost their lives.

From 8 to 16 August Park had lost ninety pilots with another fifty being wounded. Dowding needed to find pilots to plug the gaps appearing in Park's squadrons and he requested the transfer of experienced pilots from other commands as well as making a request to the Fleet Air Arm.

A growing crisis was developing in relation to the maintenance of 11 Group's airfields. Park made a strong complaint to the Air Ministry about its failure to provide sufficient men and materials to keep his airfields operational. On his own initiative he arranged for soldiers to be employed filling the craters on runways. He was adamant that if he had not taken this action a German victory would have been on the cards as early as 15 August. This was not likely to make him friends at the Air Ministry and perhaps fuelled later schisms. Dowding later recognised that Park was right and that the condition of 11 Group airfields was as serious as Park indicated. On 16 August, Park and Dowding were confronted with the hard evidence of the damage Luftwaffe raids were inflicting. Attacks on this day at Gosport, Brize Norton and Farnborough were outside 11 Group's area but Tangmere had to endure a major attack with the destruction of hangers and station buildings. Repairs had taken place to Ventnor, a vital part of the radar chain, but it was attacked again, Park ordering the installation of a mobile installation to plug the gap.

The period from 19 August to 5 September is one in which 11 Group achievements were striking. Crucially five times as many German pilots were killed as those on the British side. But this disguised the acute problem of insufficient trained pilots faced by Park. Out of a total strength of around 1,000, Fighter Command had suffered 106 killed and an equal number badly wounded. Despite this, Park worked tirelessly to achieve excellence, criticising controllers for failure to intercept the enemy experienced by 7 out of 18 of his squadrons. This he put down to their flying at 16,000 feet allowing bombers to get through at 15,000 feet. Interceptions were being made only after the enemy had bombed. Park was highly conscious of the intelligence from Dowding that German invasion Operation Sea Lion was about to happen. In anticipation of further attacks directed at the airfields Park ordered his squadrons to fall back away from the coast allowing them to achieve superior height for attack.

Such was the state of bases within 11 Group that Dowding convened a meeting with himself, Park, Nicholl of Fighter Command, Sholto Douglas and a Group Captain from the Air Ministry to examine retrenchment. Although there was a policy of gradually replacing pilots and machines in squadrons as they became depleted, the scale of the Luftwaffe attack meant that there was a real danger of their being overwhelmed. In theory pilots were available to replace those lost in 11 Group but the problem was that they were not combat ready. To disguise how badly hit 11 Group was, Dowding pledged a commitment to keep its pilot numbers up to the required number by authorising movement from other groups.

Sholto Douglas was critical of Dowding's analysis saying it was too pessimistic but Dowding replied that Park was being forced to replace a number of squadrons which had only just come into the line. Air Chief Marshall Sir Douglas Evill now intervened in support of Dowding quoting evidence that pilot casualties in the previous four weeks had totalled 348 but the Operational Training Units had managed to produce only 280 replacements. Park then outlined how 11 Group was being forced to operate with a continual shortfall and Dowding interrupted: 'We are going downhill.' Park raised concerns about having to work with understrength squadrons and pointed to the reality of having to fight while his aerodromes were being bombed. His pilots were getting little rest or proper meals due to night raids and general disorganization. The suggestion was put forward of opening another training unit and Douglas stated in defence that if the whole of August was considered the command had kept up its strength reasonably well. Evill stated that the establishment of another training unit would require the loss of experienced pilots from combat duty who would have to transfer to training activities.

By the following day Douglas was complaining that the minutes of the meeting made him appear as 'Mutt', a music hall comic who was on stage to ask silly questions, and that they misrepresented him. Evill replied to Douglas rejecting the charge against the minutes saying they were what had been taken down by the shorthand typist. Park and Dowding, who both felt Douglas had limited ability, felt that their methods of making the best possible use of limited resources were viable. In this they were supported by Evill and Nicholl who were skilled and experienced officers. This incident no doubt added to Douglas' antipathy to both Dowding and Park which would emerge at a meeting later that year on Douglas' home ground at the Air Ministry.

Park had to deal with the situation at Hawkinge where seven hangers and adjoining buildings lay in ruins; the situation for his pilots was equally bleak at Westhampnett where 145 Squadron had lost 10 of its 21 pilots. Of the 217 fighters in action on 12 August, 18 had been lost.

The next day, 13 August, radar provided Park with sufficient time to react to large numbers of enemy aircraft nearing the south coast. He scrambled two squadrons over the airfields in Suffolk as well as another two squadrons of Hurricanes and Spitfires. The objectives were the protection of a convoy in the Thames Estuary and patrols above Hawking and Manston. Park set up patrols using Tangmere's Hurricanes to protect Hawkinge and Manston with a split group on patrol in the western region in a designated periphery of Sussex from Arundel to Petworth. He employed Tangmere's Hurricanes over Canterbury where they had the flexibility to be employed in any direction where a crisis threatened. As a final move Park used a Spitfire squadron from Kenley together with another Tangmere squadron. Retaining his reserves he still had around fifty per cent of his Hurricanes uncommitted and two thirds of his Spitfires. Just how effective these dispositions were is shown by the way the Hurricanes patrolling over Canterbury and Bognor as well as near Worthing effectively intercepted the Luftwaffe before its bombers and accompanying fighters reached their targets.

In France Göring was trying to make sense of his false intelligence on the number of fighters Park possessed, and he came to the wrong conclusion that Dowding had withdrawn Hurricanes and Spitfires from the north of England. On the basis of this he ordered attacks from Luftwaffe bases in Norway and Denmark on the north-east of England, only to find these were effectively resisted by 12 and 13 Groups in possession of effective fighter resources. Again one of the strange facts of the Luftwaffe's situation is why Göring did not order a more systematic attack on the British radar as it would have brought dividends; as it was, the radar stations were quickly able to return to operations.

Park kept his controllers well informed about the progress of the battle and the lessons as he saw them from his process of attrition with the Luftwaffe. It was clear that his real vulnerability lay with his cluster of airfields which if they were taken out of action would make any resistance in the South East very difficult. In addition, the issue of night fighting was coming into prominence, with RAF Command struggling to find an adequate night fighter and the Blenheims proving incapable of performing this role effectively. Despite the Luftwaffe's poor targeting, serious attacks began on 11 Group's airfields with big raids on 13 August. Park commented, 'Had my aerodromes been put out of action the Germans would have won the Battle of Britain.'

Park was becoming seriously concerned that his resources of men and planes were wasting away. His strategy was to form and hold a defensive line with fifty per cent of his strength, keeping the rest up his sleeve. 11 Group's front line consisted of 30 squadrons while the other groups in Air Command had a total of 28 squadrons. When 11 Group had its back to the wall, other groups might be called upon to help.

On 15 August heavily escorted Stukas fell on Hawkinge airfield. As the result of bombing, communications with Dover, Rye and Foreness had been lost. Perhaps fortunately for Park the Luftwaffe bombed Croydon airfield mistaking it for Kenley. Park's fighters were outnumbered by 71 to 29 as the Luftwaffe flew 1,786 sorties. Following a surprise attack on Manston by Bf109s and dive bombers, Park expressed satisfaction at the way his defence had worked in its placement of planes defending Stuka dive bombing. There were sixteen casualties from machine gun fire, hangers were knocked out and important stores lost. Between 8 and 18 August, 154 of Park's pilots were killed, missing or gravely wounded. On 8 August he was 160 pilots short, with each squadron having to operate with three or four novices. With replacements running at only a third in December 1940, when he was posted to Flying Training Command, Park was able to comment on the reason why the replacement of trained pilots was so difficult: 'I found that flying training schools were working to two thirds capacity and were following a routine quite unaware of the grave shortage in Fighter Command.' One of his section leaders commented about the desperate efforts he had to make to induct new members of his squadrons into the reality of fighter conflict: 'I tried to take up my new pilots once or twice before putting them onto an operation team. It was like sentencing them to death if I didn't.'

One of Park's 11 Group pilots, Alan Deere, commented about how bleak August turned out to be: 'I hardly knew what I was doing. We used to fly down to Manston from Hornchurch, get bombed there, do two or three operations, get bombed again and then home in the evening if we could.' Park was being forced to raid the Fleet Air Arm and Coastal Command for pilots. On 17 August the Luftwaffe at last found Kenley and following severe bombing reduced it to a non-operational status. Between 13 and 22 August, 44 pilots were killed and 20 wounded. Despite this Park was still managing to hold four squadrons in reserve, but he felt his capacity for response was being relentlessly ground down. He stepped up his visits to his bases within 11 Group, providing a boost to his beleaguered pilots and ground crew, strengthening morale as he stepped from his Hurricane in his white flying suit.

On 18 August Park observed over 100 Luftwaffe fighters crossing the Channel from his operation room at Uxbridge. As far as Sussex and Kent were concerned, due to the intensity of the attack they were experiencing he was about to lose control of their defence. However, Park's strategy was to seek to draw off the Luftwaffe bombers' fighter escort, employing his Spitfires and leaving the bombers to the Hurricanes. On 18 August, 54 Squadron in 4 engagements shot down 14 Luftwaffe planes. Despite radar's virtues, Al Deere pointed to the inadequacy of the information it provided. 'Was it 2 bombers or 30 bombers – there was no way of telling. It was blind folly to hurl our planes at an indefinite object.' Poor weather conditions restricted German attacks but provided Park with an opportunity for airfield repairs. On the other side, the Germans were able to organise a more effectively targeted attack on the airfields of the South East.

Chapter 14

Into the Crucial Stage – 24 August to 6 September

The third phase – again the dates are debated – saw a change in the focus of the Luftwaffe attacks on more inland targets. The targets now were aerodromes and factories. The Luftwaffe had now organised itself into smaller formations with the fighters pulled closer in to the main flight. At this point, Hitler believed that British surrender was a possibility and efforts were made to drop leaflets as 'The last appeal for reason'. On 7 August Kesselring's Luftflotte 2 flying from airfields in France, Belgium and Holland were given targets west from Portsmouth to Bristol and into South Wales. 'The invasion of England cannot go ahead till England is without its air force,' Göring is reported saying as plans were put in place for major attacks on 10 August. Fortunately for Park, Major Weather intervened in the form of cloud and rain so that he was able to use the pause in attacks for airfield repairs and repairs to his aircraft. 'It's quiet but at least I've managed to re-establish my airfields, but the blighters are up to something,' Park commented to Dowding.

Park also expressed his frustration that despite his order to squadrons that they should concentrate on Luftwaffe bombers, Spitfires were accounting for only half the downed Bf109s, suggesting that the Hurricanes and Defiants were engaging them too. Against this, here was proof the Hurricane and Defiant airmen could strike back effectively against formations of Messerschmitts. Park's new directive said, 'We must now drop the practice of detailing a portion of our fighters to go high to engage fighter escort. These squadrons merely get drawn off and permit the bombers with their very close escort to proceed unhindered. All squadrons dispatched against raids of 30 or more are to be detailed to engage the bomber formation. I've given a height of about 2,000 feet above the reported height of the enemy bomber formations.' Other frustrations were evident; Park held Leigh-Mallory personally responsible for failing to prevent the saturation bombing of North Weald. His anger was only second to that of the airfield Wing Commander whose voice had roared out from the airfield's loudspeakers during the raid: 'Any officer, NCO or airmen who leaves his post of duty is a coward and rat – I shoot rats on sight.'

At a time when everything seemed black for Fighter Command, Bomber Command intervened on their behalf. Churchill ordered a retaliation for the Luftwaffe's bombing of parts of outer London. On the evening of 25 August, eighty-one British bombers commenced their long flight to Berlin. Crews with specialist skills in navigation had been chosen. When they reached Berlin it was under heavy cloud cover; they dispatched twenty tonnes of bombs on what was taken to be the city when in reality it was just its outskirts. In practical terms the raid was a failure but its psychological effect on the German High Command was profound. For Göring the result was a serious loss in prestige, and as a consequence there was a radical change in German strategy.

On 26 August Park introduced the 310 Czechoslovakian Squadron with twelve of the unit's Hurricanes attacking the Germans south west of Colchester. On 24 August Manston and Hornchurch airfields were attacked as well as North Weald suffering serious damage. Park requested support from 12 Group to provide cover for his airfields north of the Thames. Only one squadron turned up, Leigh-Mallory having wasted precious time in organizing his Big Wing formation.

On 26 August Fighter Command proved that it was far from finished. Although the new tactics of the Germans had surprised Park with their long trail of aircraft dominated by fighters, Park had succeeded in responding effectively. It was 11 Group's problem of achieving any sort of integration with 12 Group that created the difficulties. On 27 August Park called together his controllers and sector commanders and openly accused Leigh-Mallory of deliberately neglecting his role in protecting 11 Group's bases and airfields. In contrast he heaped praise on the support he had been offered by 10 Group: 'Thanks to the coordination offered by 10 Group, they are always prepared to detail 2 or 4 squadrons. Up to date 12 Group on the other hand have not shown the same desire to cooperate by dispatching their squadrons to the place requested. The result of this attitude has been that on 2 occasions recently when 12 Group offered assistance and were requested by us to patrol our aerodromes, their squadrons did not in fact patrol over our aerodromes. On both these occasions our aerodromes were heavily bombed. As acceptance of direct offers from 12 Group have not resulted in their squadrons being placed where we had requested, controllers are now requested to put their requests to controller Fighter Command.'

There was another big challenge: five of his six air bases had been extensively damaged and Lympne and Manston were unfit for operational use. Biggin Hill would be out of action for more than a week. After bombing, although alternative forms of communication were being found, in many cases these were not adequate to cope with the three squadrons operating out of a sector. All this added to his task of commanding the RAF's front line response to the German air offensive, and it was unrelenting.

At the beginning of August, aircraft activity on both sides has been described as taking each day as it came, with Luftflotte 2 and Fliegerkorps 8 carrying out mine laying activities with sporadic attacks on ships in the Channel. However, by 21 July Göring had given the order that Fighter Command should be completely destroyed.

The whole tempo changed with a vengeance around *Adlertag* which commenced on 13 August, and saw 1,485 German sorties to which Park responded with 727 sorties. The ongoing Luftwaffe problem of poor intelligence meant that it hit minor targets like Eastchurch and Detling missing Farnborough and Rochford. Again on 16 August attacks aimed at fighter bases only reached three of them: Manston, West Malling and Tangmere. It was on this day that Park recommended Flight Lieutenant James Nicolson for a Victoria Cross for remaining in his burning plane in a cockpit filling with smoke and flames and yet still managing to shoot down another Luftwaffe aircraft before bailing out.

On 18 August the major attack on Kenley resulted in the destruction of ten hangers containing Hurricanes. Attacks on this day also included the Isle of Wight and parts of Kent. On 30 August these attacks began to include sector stations in what some commentators believe were the heaviest attacks of the entire Battle. Better German targeting saw attacks on the Vauxhall factory at Luton, and bomber production at Radnett was seriously disrupted. On the following day 39 aircraft were lost and 14 pilots killed following attacks on Kent, the Thames Estuary, Debden, North Weald, Duxford and Croydon. Finally after sustaining a number of bombing raids Biggin Hill was forced to close and move to small sector stations in their vicinity. On 19 August Park gave instructions that his aircraft were not to be vectored over the sea by flight controllers because 'too many pilots were being drowned after ditching.'

The German belief that Fighter Command had been forced to move pilots and aircraft from the north (mentioned in the last chapter) meant that

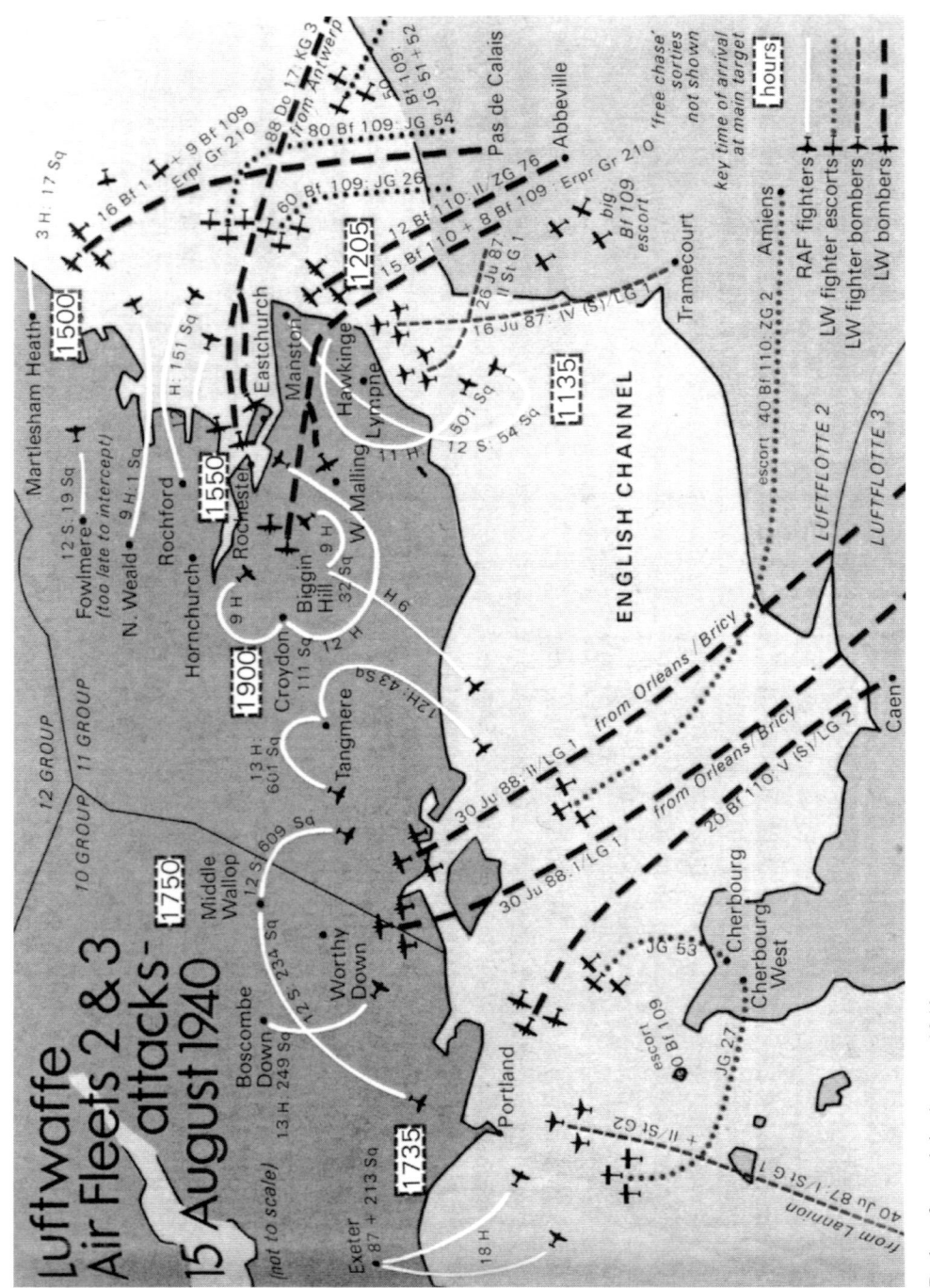

Paths of attack in August 1940.

throughout August and September they misjudged the resources Park had at his disposal. Not until later in the month did the Luftwaffe seriously attack key bases like Kenley and Biggin Hill concentrating on minor coastal command centres such as Detling. Luftwaffe thinking was coloured by 11 Group scrambling just twenty fighters on 15 August against the 125 launched by the Luftwaffe. On this day on a visit with Lord Ismay to Uxbridge, Churchill had bellowed to him as he sought to comment: 'Don't talk to me. Never before have I been so moved.' Later he produced the famous quote, 'Never in the field of human conflict has so much been owed by so many to so few.'

In the Luftwaffe ranks there was dissension, with Deichmann ordering a full attack on 15 August without Göring's permission. Göring was also incensed that suburbs of London had been bombed (as described) against his instructions. Nor were the RAF immune to argument about the tactics to be followed. Luftwaffe attacks on some 11 Group bases were beginning to highlight Park's need for support from 12 Group.

Eagle Day on 13 August has tended to be regarded by some historians as a day of British victory. Churchill reported to Cabinet that losses amounted to thirteen, when in fact there were three more. If the whole period from 13 to 15 August is taken into account, it reveals an RAF loss of fifty-eight aircraft and nine others returning to their base with serious damage.

On 16 August Park had just 430 operational aircraft, but the Luftwaffe's real advantage was having 1,560 pilots compared to Park's 1,380. By 17 August Park had received 70 pilots to replace the 68 killed or missing. At Duxford 310 Czech Squadron had become operational.

At midday on 18 August the Luftwaffe had attacked 11 Group's key bases at Kenley and Biggin Hill. Further attacks on the 30th and 31st were sustained causing substantial damage and the station commanders prepared for the destruction of the remaining buildings. The first attack on Croydon took place employing Bf110 aircraft, part of the crack *Erprobungsgruppe* led by Rubensdörffer. Large-scale raids were planned on southern England, the first at 1300 hours. Two Hurricane squadrons forced their way through the escorts and caught a group of dive bombers about to attack Thorney Island. In short order Hurricanes shot down three Ju87s. Hurricane pilot Flight Lieutenant Frank Carey commented how these dive bombers were difficult to hit in their dive, but 'they could not dive forever' and became vulnerable for attack.

Attacks took place on Gosport and Ford and the radar at Poling. The twenty-five miles between Bognor Regis and Gosport became the theatre for a mass dogfight with 300 aircraft thrusting, twisting, and turning. From 602 squadron twelve Spitfires caught up with a group of Stukas just as they were leaving Britain at Middleton-on-Sea causing many of them to crash into the sea. Fighter Ace Bob Doe of 234 Squadron spotted Messerschmitts attacking barrage balloons around Portsmouth and chased one of the aircraft across the Channel watching the German pilot bale out of his doomed aircraft. The whole contest took six minutes. On that day the Luftwaffe lost 69 aircraft either crashed or damaged beyond repair. Fighter Command's losses were 31 aircraft with 7 destroyed on the ground.

When Park received intelligence of another attack on Biggin Hill he scrambled 111 Squadron who harassed the Luftwaffe bombers so that their bombs missed the airfield; but they hit the surrounding residential area causing a large number of fatalities. German bombers were more successful in attacks on 26 August and 23 September, hitting the control tower and one of the hangers. Debden's first attack was on 10 July when the Luftwaffe achieved little damage. A more serious raid occurred on 26 August when a communication failure by Fighter Command caused them to lose contact with the incoming bombers resulting in 100 high explosive and incendiary bombs destroying the airmen's quarters, the NAAFI and the sergeants' mess through direct hits. There were five deaths when the hail of bombs made a direct hit on the trench where ground staff were sheltering. Following this, Park ordered the reinforcement of Debden's Eagle Squadron No 71, to protect the airfield. 71 was formed in September 1940, the other Eagle Squadrons in 1941. The sector station at Hawkinge hosted almost one third of the 11 Group squadrons during the course of the battle, most squadrons spending at least a day there. Two squadrons, 79 and 245, were based there but other squadrons were often forced to land there either through lack of fuel or as a result of damage. Hawkinge experienced its first raid on 12 August resulting in the loss of many buildings, its number 3 hanger and equipment storeroom and extensive loss of any vehicles caught in the open. Remarkably the operations room and many aircraft at Hawkinge survived. Park was kept in contact with his principal airfield staff and the army who were working through the night to maintain a link with Uxbridge.

Following action on 28 August, Peter Townsend of 85 Squadron commented about the problem of getting to the bombers through the inevitable fighter escort: 'There is only one way and that was to prepare for a head-on collision and veer at the last moment,' he said. Manston suffered a major raid on 24 August resulting in so much damage that Park ordered the evacuation of all essential personnel. Despite this, repairs were quickly made to the grass runway and it was only out of use for short periods even though the buildings supporting the airfield were out of use. Park received intelligence that the Germans believed the damage to Manston was irreparable.

Park became aware that the Germans had changed their tactics, their fighters now flying at the same altitude as their bombers. He believed this placed a greater responsibility on the Observer Corps and formation leaders to provide detail of the height of the attacking aircraft. He summed up the growing desperate situation: 'Contrary to general belief and official reports the enemy bombing by day did extensive damage to 5 of our forward aerodromes and also 6 of our 7 support airfields. Manston and Lympne will be unfit for operations for days and Biggin Hill's damage means it can only support a single squadron. If the Luftwaffe continues their present all-out attack the sector airfields defending London will be in a parlous state.' He continued his argument with the Air Ministry about the inadequate resources made available to him to repair damaged airfields.

Chapter 15

The Battle goes on

To make matters worse for Park, Leigh-Mallory's 12 Group began to agitate about how he could have been used to greater effect, and claimed that the squadrons attached to 12 Group were being deliberately excluded from the conflict. One of his young pilots, Hugh Dundas, describes sitting on the ground in his plane while a life and death conflict was taking place in the 11 Group area. There were claims that appeals for help from 11 Group arrived too late for 12 Group to make an effective intervention. Park countered by saying that this was because they were taking too long to assemble in a formation before going into action.

Since large-scale attacks had commenced on 8 August, the Luftwaffe had lost 350 aircraft. It was slowly dawning on Göring that the RAF was a far tougher nut to crack than he had imagined. Said Churchill: 'The gratitude of every home in our island, in our Empire, and indeed throughout the world, except in the abodes of the guilty, goes out to the British airmen who, undaunted by odds, unwearied in their constant challenge and mortal danger, are turning the tide of the World War by their prowess and devotion... All our hearts go out to the fighter pilots, whose brilliant action we see with our own eyes day after day.'

But on 19 August there was a staff conference. In attendance were Air Chief Marshal Dowding and the commanders of each of the Fighter Command groups. Park was at pains to highlight how crucial it was to defend 11 Group airfields and in particular Kenley and Biggin Hill: 'Now Göring knows he can penetrate our inner airfields there will be no stopping him from continuing,' he told the conference. Nowhere on the British side was the crisis more evident than in 11 Group, under the heaviest pressure from the armada Göring was now sending against them. Although impressive results had been achieved it seemed impossible to quell the German attacks. Attacks against crucial airbases at Kenley, Lympne, Hawkinge, Manston, Martlesham, Rochester and Croydon had underlined the group's vulnerability. Essentially a war of attrition was developing and Park was fully aware that the resources available to him might not be enough. The debit side was showing 211 single-engine fighters lost and 154 experienced pilots. Dowding was asking himself: 'In a month's time, how many pilots and aircraft will I have at my disposal?'

Park was well aware of the psychology behind many of his pilots being drawn into combat with other fighters and preferring this to the essential task of shooting down German bombers. Fighter-to-fighter combat was costing too many pilots' lives and destroying too many aircraft while German bombers were penetrating British targets.

Park published Directive Number 4:

- Use fighter aircraft to attack the large enemy formations over land or close enough to land for our own fighters to be able to glide to the coast if they are damaged. For the next two or three weeks, we cannot afford to lose pilots through ditching in the sea.
- Avoid sending fighters out over the sea to hunt reconnaissance aircraft or small formations of enemy fights.
- Dedicate a couple of fighters to tackle occasional reconnaissance aircraft that come over the land. If it is cloudy keep the patrol of one or two fighters up over any airfield that the enemy can approach through the clouds.
- For major incursions towards land only a limited number of squadrons equipped with Spitfires will be deployed against enemy fighters. Our primary purpose is to attack the enemy bombers, especially those which fly under the cloud base.
- If our squadrons around London are airborne attacking large hostile raids, support from 12 Group should be sought to resist large flights of enemy raiders as well as for protection of stations north and east of London such as Debden, North Weald and Hornchurch.
- If a large raid has crossed the coast and is approaching our airfields, send up a squadron, or even the sector's own training group, to patrol over each sector station.

At this conference Air Vice-Marshal Leigh-Mallory brought forward his argument in favour of Big Flight response to attacks from the Luftwaffe. This was possibly the first time he had done so in a forum of this nature, although he had already been putting his views forward in confidence to other members of the Air Ministry. It was pointed out to him by Dowding that the 11 Group area covering the South East was too large for the large flights envisaged to form up in time to offer valid resistance. Dowding said that the concept would seriously weaken existing plans to offer a coherent defence and that sending up as many as five squadrons might represent a catastrophe in terms of lost aircraft and pilots.

Park spoke of the need to prevent pilots seeking conflict with Bf109s and 110s when they should be attacking bombers. The fact was the Luftwaffe fighters were operating on limited fuel which gave them less than thirty minutes over England. 'Prime targets are the bomber formations and fighter combat must be avoided if bombers are present,' Park told the conference.

Dowding emphasised the need for Groups 10 and 12 to offer support to Park. There was a discussion of the tactics that should be used in conflicts with Luftwaffe fighters. Park highlighted the dangers of being 'jumped' by Bf109s and 110s, the possibility that Göring might bring escorting fighters down to the height of incoming bombers, or that the German bombers might fly higher with their escorts.

Park had not been won over by the argument about the vulnerability of his coastal airfields at Lympne, Hawkinge and Manston. He felt that his Directive 4 had corrected some of the mistakes 11 Group had been making. The plans were for it to be used to attack vessels in the Channel during an invasion. At the same time a tense Göring was issuing orders that the Ju87 dive bombers would be withdrawn from the campaign. He was at odds with his commanders in that he wanted his Bf109s and 110s not to be linked to bombers but to have free movement to seek out British fighters and engage them. 'We must dispatch as many fighters as possible on free hunting, which allows them to provide with an indirect cover since they then operate under the most ideal conditions to combat enemy fighters,' he told his commanders. From then on, his Messerschmitts would play a leading role in attacks on the RAF. Because of the long flights and the fuel involved in attacking from their base on the Cotentin Peninsula he would transfer his fighter unit Luftflotte 3 to the Pas de Calais. Luftwaffe 3 would now switch to the night bombing of British bomber bases. Bombing during the day would be carried out by small units from Luftflotte 2. There would now be an extension to ground targets and aviation industries around London. His tactic was to employ smaller flights of bombers but with a large presence of Bf109 and 110 fighters. With these directives Göring set in motion the scenario for the crucial period of the Battle of Britain.

The New Zealand ace Alan Deere wrote about the almost impossible odds faced by fighter squadrons in relation to Park's tactic of maintaining large reserves of fighters in these months of August and September. But he believed that however difficult it was to draw off the accompanying Luftwaffe escort fighters for Spitfire squadrons like the one at Hornchurch, it was exactly the right policy. 'I strongly support this view,' he said. 'On numerous occasions I witnessed the majority of their escorts set upon Hurricanes, which excellent as they are could not have coped without the intervention of Spitfires.' It was views like that of Deere that Park received as he flew around in his Hurricane visiting the airfields in his group.

Now a period of relative quiet occurred where both sides appeared to be taking stock of the situation they found themselves in, with strategic moves such as Göring moving his fighter base to Calais and closer to the British coast. However from 26 August Park's concern about what the Luftwaffe were up to was answered with more mass attacks. He quickly realised that rather than flying at 20,000 feet and above a bomber flight the Bf109s and 110s were now flying at the same height as the incoming bombers at 10-15,000 feet. Park was struggling despite this to get an accurate picture of the height and strength of German attacks, and because of the size of the attack had to release half his fighters at once for the first time, having the other half at standby.

On the following day Park had taken advantage of the bad weather to make contact with his controllers to call a meeting with the leading figures in the RAF in the presence of Air Commander Sholto Douglas. At the meeting, Leigh-Mallory stepped up his advocacy of a tactical change involving the deployment of Big Wings. He had maintained his resentment of being passed over for control of the pivotal 11 Group which he considered was his as a matter of right since the announcement of Park's appointment. Since February 1940 he had begun to conspire against Dowding to have him removed as Air Chief Marshal. Park recalls: 'Leigh-Mallory came out of Dowding's office, paused in mine and said in my presence that he would move heaven and earth to get Dowding removed from Fighter Command, and he made it quite clear to me that he was jealous of my Group that was now in the front line.'

During the meeting Park had set out his reasons for saying that Leigh-Mallory's advocacy of Big Wing was both impractical and unrealistic.

The Big Wing concept seemed to be mainly justified on the basis of the psychological boost it provided to those defending against Luftwaffe attack. For pilots it might provide reassurance that they were not fighting against impossible odds. Secondly there was the claim that it was the appearance of large flights to defend London that prompted Hitler to cease his attempt to achieve dominance by air of Britain. Park cited an example that had occurred the previous day of large numbers of Dorniers approaching from the east and how he had contacted 12 Group for an interception before they fell on 11 Group airfields. This appeal had come to nothing. He compared this with the way his 310 Squadron had been able to make an interception on the coast.

'When the weather was fine, and conditions ideal for flying, it concerned us if the enemy decided not to launch an attack on us. We would wonder as to what they were up to. Everyone would come up with suggestions as to why it was so unusually quiet, but no one really knew,' Park commented. He barely suppressed his anger when he heard that during the third raid of 28 August seven squadrons were lured into combat over the Channel despite his express instructions not to operate in this way. Six Bf109s were destroyed but five Hurricanes and Spitfires were shot down. Park again emphasised that there should be no attacks of Luftwaffe fighters operating without bombers unless they constituted a genuine threat to airfields or aircraft factories. In addition Park issued orders that his pilots should immediately report the height of German flights. But at the end of this day the decisive action against Fighter Command had not been achieved despite 576 sorties by the Germans. He believed that the Bf109 was a much superior aircraft to the Hurricane. That night while Liverpool burned Blenheim night fighters searched in vain for the Heinkels and Junkers alternatively bombing and departing.

The following day Park wrote to Evill commending by comparison the support he had received from Sir Quintin Brand of 10 Group and the way that his controllers at his airfields complained about the uncertainty of any support from 12 Group in the event of attack. There was an inherent difficulty in being able to check what 12 Group was doing following the issue of a request for support. He had belatedly received a report of 12 Group fighters patrolling North Weald, Debden and Hornchurch after they had been severely bombed.

Meanwhile Göring was fretting at his paltry results from 700 fighter sorties with victories reported amounting to just fifteen. Based on this result Göring decided to place more emphasis on the Bf110 than the Bf109.

On 30 August there were 1,345 sorties as Göring threw everything he had towards the destruction of Fighter Command. This was the heaviest day of fighting Park had experienced so far. At 10.30 am Park saw the first main raid come in over Kent and Sussex. This was followed at 1.30

pm by waves of bombers targeting southern Kent and at 4 pm the largest raid of the day. It was the commencement of eight consecutive days of concentrated attacks on Fighter Command airfields. Göring had promised Hitler he would only need five days to finish off Fighter Command. Fighter Command's morale remained high throughout these mass attacks while in the Luftwaffe it was described as being rock bottom. Göring blamed the inadequacy of his own pilots for the loss of 800 aircraft. In reality a war of attrition was beginning to develop with depleted resources of men and machines on both sides. 'Göring had us nearly on our knees, not quite but nearly,' Park admitted.

Despite Park's policy of rotating squadrons to quieter areas and holding back more experienced pilots, raids were causing more and more damage, with communication with bases from Dover to Rye being destroyed. The death toll rose steadily to forty with frequent sweeps by Bf110s and 109s designed to lure Park into a commitment to fighter combat. In practice, squadron commanders struggled to break through covering fighters to the bombers to such an extent that this sometimes involved a head-on collision with the invaders. By 1145 hours a second group of Luftwaffe fighters and bombers had crossed the coast and were attacked by squadrons 85, 111, 222, and 616. Park then released sixteen squadrons, but many pilots had difficulty achieving sufficient height to make an attack. The skies above Surrey and Kent were dotted with dogfighting aircraft. At 1400 hours Park was faced with a Luftwaffe attack directed at the Thames Estuary so he scrambled 56 Squadron at North Weald, 79 Squadron at Biggin Hill, and 225 Squadron at Hornchurch, marking the second time that day he had all his aircraft in operation. At 1800 hours Biggin Hill was bombed for the second time that day with destruction of its communication links and the cratering of its runways. Park received intelligence that nine Ju88s had penetrated at low level resulting in the deaths of 39 and the injury of 35. Throughout the day thirty-two squadrons had been in action resulting in thirty-nine aircraft being destroyed and the deaths of fifty RAF personnel. The Germans had suffered the loss of forty-one fighters. For the second time that day there was another attack on Biggin Hill when nine Ju88 bombers got through British defences in a low level bombing attack using 1,000 lb bombs. The transport yard was destroyed, storerooms, the armoury and both the sergeants' and officers' messes were wrecked and yet another hanger was laid waste. Thirty-nine personnel were killed and thirty-five wounded.

The 30th of August proved a difficult day for Park for by 1030 hours sixty Bf109s crossed the coast meaning there was likely to be no respite from bombing at Kenley. This was made worse by a lucky hit on communication cabling knocking out seven radar stations and Park complaining of being 'blind' for some of the day.

The 31st of August dawned with all G11 airfields having already experienced some degree of damage as the Luftwaffe put together an even larger operation. Clear strains were developing, reflecting days of bombing that had been experienced. For instance Debden was hit by one hundred bombs. Despite Beaverbrook's replacement programme Park was losing more aircraft than could be replaced. Park repeatedly issued his key instruction that as far as possible there should be no fighter-to-fighter conflict. The toll of squadron leaders was increasingly meaning that fighter squadron leadership devolved to younger inexperienced pilots. On 31 August, as a consequence of heavy bombing of Biggin Hill, Park was forced to close the base and withdraw his squadrons to other bases. This coincided with Fighter Command suffering its worst day of losses of any day of the conflict, a total of thirty-nine. This was the day Dowding had to recognise the failure of his Defiant aircraft and withdraw them from fighter daylight operations.

Dowding now acknowledged that Fighter Command was losing aircraft and pilots faster than it was possible to replace them. On a single day 39 aircraft were shot down and 14 pilots killed. Over the last ten days of August Fighter Command lost 126 fighter pilots. Park had appealed to 12 Group without any response on several occasions. When bombs began falling on Biggin Hill he lost his temper: 'Where the hell were your fighters that were supposed to be protecting my airfields?' he said in a telephone call. Leigh-Mallory's reply made him more angry when he claimed his pilots had not been able to find the German raiders. 'Listen,' he shouted down the phone, 'your fighters were not supposed to look for the enemy – they should have been above southern London airfields, waiting for the enemy.'

As well as attacks on Biggin Hill, Croydon and Eastchurch suffered bombing as well. Kesselring was ordering repeated waves into the attack. At Kenley, Tangmere and Shoreham, bombing was occurring. Most worrying for Park was that a raid on an electricity generation plant resulted in the radar stations at Beachy Head, Dover, Fairlight, Foreness, Pevensey, Rye and Whitstable being put out of action. Biggin Hill was out of action and its sector control function was moved by Park to Hornchurch. There was evidence that Göring's tactic of sending over vast numbers of aircraft was beginning to work. Park's analysis resulted in his repeating his earlier instruction to commanders that his fighter pilots should as a matter of urgency report height, strength and composition to their operations room to provide a clearer picture of the incoming raiders.

Park was now very much aware he faced a deepening crisis. As far as 11 Group's airfields were concerned, a courier sent to report on the state of Kenley and Biggin Hill returned with the comment, 'It was like a slaughter house.'

Hazel Gregory from Sleaford, now approaching 90, then 18, was an aircraftswoman working as a plotter in the 11 Group bunker at Uxbridge during the Battle of Britain: 'I never had time to think what would happen if the German bombers got through. I was once at the Watford end of the table and remember one 400-aircraft raid – you couldn't see the surface of the plotting table it was so covered with movements. That day I remember Sir Keith talking about bringing a 'Big Wing' from 12 Group to help out and they smashed through the formation of enemy aircraft.' She has a vivid recollection of Park's omnipresence: 'I remember him well – he was always there making decision after decision. He was a lovely man – he used to bring us girls bags of liquorice allsorts.'

September the 1st and the new month opened with Luftwaffe pressure on 11 Group airfields and radar stations along the south coast. Park was aware that he would be putting even more pressure on his already exhausted pilots whom he had asked to carry out around 2,000 sorties in the space of just thirty-six hours in the last two days of August.

Park's problem was if he scrambled too early, his squadrons would be over water and for shot-down pilots there was only a thirty per cent chance of their being saved. On the other hand if he was too late the Luftwaffe would almost certainly reach their target. Further, if he scrambled too many there would be insufficient aircraft to protect his airfields.

The day was a bleak one for the RAF. Serious damage took place at Biggin Hill, Eastchurch and Detling. At 1400 hours Biggin Hill was experiencing yet another raid, its sixth in three days. One of these disrupted the funeral service for the fifty at the airfield killed in an earlier raid.

Two of the airfield's ground staff, Elspeth Henderson and Sergeant Helen Turner, were recognised for the way they stayed at their post and worked through the heavy bombing, receiving the Military Medal.

September had come and Kesselring's undertaking to break Fighter Command before the beginning of the month had come and gone.

But the Luftwaffe continued its brutal attacks focused on Biggin Hill, Detling, and Eastchurch the following day. Short Brothers works at Rochester and the Vickers factory at Brooklands was bombed. The skies above England were darkened with scores of Bf109s and 110s seeking to draw Fighter Command into combat. Park scrambled eleven squadrons.

At North Weald the tough ground crew were taken aback by the nonchalant attitude of the pilots from 249 Squadron apparently unaware of the seriousness of the challenge they faced. 'They strolled casually out to the aircraft while the ground crew stood by them, engines running, waiting in disbelief,' observed Eric Clayton. 249 Squadron had just arrived as replacement for the run-down 56 and 151 Squadrons. Unfortunately they failed to realise that 10 Group enjoyed the advantage of considerable distance enabling them to gain height over the Luftwaffe – an advantage they would not enjoy in 11 Group.

The 2nd of September turned out to be one of the worst days for the Luftwaffe. They lost twenty-one Bf 109s while four staggered back to their base with combat damage. In reply Fighter Command had lost twenty-four fighters although ten were repairable.

Between 4 and 6 September both sides were suffering from exhaustion and Park was conscious that his capability for resistance was being worn down. Despite this, and no matter what the condition of squadrons, he asked them to come forward and they had to be thrown into the Battle. Perhaps 54 Squadron illustrates most clearly the crisis in experienced manpower. Although it boasted ninety-two victories since July, only four of its original pilots had survived. Despite this there were complaints from the squadron about being moved to C category which effectively took the squadron out of active combat.

Lord Beaverbrook contacted Park about the consequence of the raids on Brooklands (Vickers Armstrong) and Rochester (Short Brothers). To keep up the rate of production at Brooklands he ordered the movement of aspects of manufacturing to requisitioned private houses.

But it was again the raids on Park's airfields that caused him greatest concern. Francis K. Mason in his *Battle over Britain* writes of Fighter Command's 'nervous and physical exhaustion'. Park also knew his ground organization was being bled badly. He repeatedly pointed out how the destruction of his sector stations would mean he would be forced to hit out like a blind man against the Luftwaffe. Only some of the leaders of Air Command recognised that Park was being asked to defend the existence of Fighter Command almost single-handedly.

Biggin Hill now had only enough resources to support a single squadron. Richard Grive, the sector commander, was so demoralised by the consequence of repeated bombing that he had his last remaining hangar blown up. Park ordered his court martial but the popular Grive, a First World War ace, was acquitted.

Park on his regular visits to his sectors could not avoid a change in demeanour, as described by historian Larry Foster: 'They were a sorry looking lot. Scruffy, listless, they were quarrelling among themselves over trivialities, drinking hard but entirely without zest. Over the last few weeks they have taken a severe mauling. Two of the sergeants were bad twitch cases, regularly reporting sick to avoid flying. They complained of stomach aches, back aches, stiff necks and other ailments which the MO could not dismiss because there were no visible symptoms. One of these men has some excuse for his edginess – only a few weeks ago he had his legs peppered with shrapnel from a Bf110 cannon.'

On 3 September Göring met his commanders in The Hague. The meeting coincided with Hitler's decision to postpone 'S' day, the launch of Operation Sea Lion, from 15 September to possibly the 21st. Göring believed that Hitler did not believe the Luftwaffe was ready for the necessary support for an invasion. There were differences between Kesselring and Sperrle but Kesselring realised he would now get his all-out attack on London. He argued that Park and Dowding would withdraw to the northern airfields following the destruction of Biggin Hill, which would pose real problems for the Luftwaffe because of the Bf109s' limited fuel capacity. By attacking London he felt sure the RAF would have to commit its limited resources to its defence. Sperrle argued against intelligence suggesting that Fighter Command was in a drastically reduced state. Kesselring believed that the attacks on Fighter Command's bases and sector airfields had not succeeded. He believed that the only way to destroy Fighter Command was in the air. Göring had previously claimed that no bombs would fall on Berlin. However, Allied bombing had taken place so there was justification for an attack on London which had been originally ruled out by Hitler.

Hitler's speech in Berlin on 4 September was to change not only the course of the Battle of Britain but also the war. 'The British will now see that we shall pay back a hundredfold,' he said, referring to the bombing attacks on Berlin. Sure enough, mindful of autumn rapidly approaching, the Luftwaffe halted its attacks on Fighter Command's ground organization on 7 September and began to target London. The good fortune of bad weather and the decision to cease attacks on Park's sectors gave him a vital few days for rebuilding runways and strengthening communication systems. Although Göring is associated with this change of direction in Luftwaffe tactics to begin bombing London, there is some evidence to suggest he was opposed to an attack on London, saying that the main focus should remain on attacks on 11 Group airfields and communications installations. He did not support the view held within the German High Command that an attack on London would destroy British morale.

Chapter 16

The Tide begins to turn

On 7 September German strategy changed radically, with a bomber force attacking London for the first time. At 5 pm Park was involved in a conference at Bentley Priory when information came through that a huge daylight attack had been launched against London. This consisted of 348 bombers escorted by 600 fighters targeting the London docks and their adjoining warehouses. The attack also targeted heavily populated streets. This was the moment for Leigh-Mallory and Douglas Bader's Big Wing as they were scrambled for patrol over London. By 16:30 hours twenty-one squadrons of Spitfires and Hurricanes had been scrambled. The first British fighter attack was east of London just after five o'clock. At 17.15 hours bombs were falling on Woolwich. Most of the 300 tons of bombs and thousands of incendiary bombs falling on London were targeted at the Victoria and Albert Docks, the West India Docks and the Surrey Commercial Docks. The attack was over in fifty minutes. Park had to recognise that the attack on London on 7 September represented a defeat not just for 11 Group but for Fighter Command as all the German bombers returned to their bases. No German flights had been repulsed by Fighter Command, and of the 268 Hurricanes and Spitfires in combat with German raiders, 44 had been shot down. In contrast German losses amounted to only 26, representing only 2 per cent of the attacking German flights. Kesselring's armada, consisting of 317 bombers and 617 fighters, made their appearance on the British radar at 4.15 pm flying at 23,000 feet spread out over a twenty-mile front.

When on 8 September Park scrambled four squadrons after German bombers were first sighted to meet an overwhelming mass of Bf109s headed to bomb East London, six aircraft were shot down with the fighter crews hardly seeing a German bomber. On the following day, 9 September, Park was able to organise a better-coordinated defence despite losing seventeen aircraft and six having to crash land. Park had to watch in frustration as repeated German attacks decimated targeted areas of London.

Park returned to Uxbridge and travelled from there to Northolt taking off in his Hurricane to fly over the blazing East End so he could assess for himself the extent of the carnage. Despite what he was observing he realised that Göring's switch of target provided him with precious space to repair his airfield infrastructure. One fact would become crystal clear when the Luftwaffe returned that night: Fighter Command had no effective answer to night raids. There was little anti-aircraft fire and little progress had been made in the development of a night fighter to challenge the Luftwaffe.

On 11 September Park called a meeting of his sector controllers and commanders. Göring's tactic of 19 August of deploying large concentrations of fighters had effectively swamped the small packets of fighters Park was able to scramble. Park now ordered that squadrons should be scrambled in pairs, preferably one squadron of Hurricanes for the bomber and one of Spitfires for the fighter escort. In addition he asked his sector commanders to put up two additional pairs of squadrons at fifteen-minute intervals. At around 15:45 hours on that day a large concentration of aircraft appeared on British radar and Park in response placed his pairs of squadrons on standby. He also scrambled the first of them. Park struggled to analyse the fighting of this Wednesday, but mistakes had been made by his controllers at Northolt and Hornchurch by putting their squadrons up at too low a level. Park's dissatisfaction was that despite the full involvement of 12 Group and the loss of many planes, only a few German planes had been shot down.

The situation began to change. From observer points at Rochford, Reigate, Rochester and Shepney came reports than the German fighter units were heading back towards the Channel at treetop level. Park acknowledged two factors at work. Firstly the unexpected level of opposition, and secondly the fighters had used up more fuel than anticipated. It took only ten minutes for the picture of the battle to profoundly change. Despite the exaggerated claims by the Germans of British losses, amounting to thirty fighters, the results of the fighting on the 11th could enable Park to have some confidence in the future course of the Battle, notwithstanding his pilots' own exaggerated claims. Nevertheless, serious damage was inflicted on the Supermarine Spitfire factory in Southampton after being first sighted at 4 pm by the Observer Corps.

It was becoming obvious not only to Park but to the Germans as well that every day that passed Fighter Command was recovering and even becoming stronger. The four quiet days of inclement weather had assisted this process. The 15th of September, now referred to as 'Battle of Britain Day', dawned bright and sunny with Mrs Churchill joining Park in the gallery of the operations room at Uxbridge. Park, having some intimation from Ultra about large scale attacks in the offing, had brought his squadrons to 'readiness'. Göring's plans were for a morning and afternoon major attack on London. This time there were no feints from the Germans hoping to draw Park's aircraft into dogfights. German strategists were advocating a tight formation for their attacking flights with the accompanying escort staying closely beside the bombers. The problem with this was that the accompanying Bf100s were forced to use up too much fuel while circling above their bombers. To add to the slow advance, there was a prevailing headwind to be contended with. This was a day Churchill chose to visit Park's headquarters at Uxbridge. Park had sent requests to 10 Group for fighters from Middle Wallop and also to Leigh-Mallory for his Duxford Wing who were to patrol at 20,000 feet above Hornchurch. Separately he scrambled the Polish 302 Squadron whose individualist approach to battle did not fit in well with Big Wing tactics. Meanwhile the Dornier bombers were continuing to make their way along the Thames Estuary with only a lonely bomber having been attacked. It was riddled with bullets but on autopilot after all its crew had bailed out; nine British pilots claimed it as a victory. Above London the Duxford flight confronted the newly-arrived Germans. Bader gave instructions for his Spitfires to climb towards the escorting Bf109s above them and for the Hurricanes to pounce on the Dorniers.

The Germans were surprised at the large number of British fighters they had suddenly been confronted with. The German aircrew had been told that these were the last fifty Spitfires. In the afternoon the German attack was met by eleven squadrons from 11 Group, several units from 10 Group, and the entire Duxford wing who attacked the incoming Bf109s from superior height. Those fighters who got to the German bombers were initially held off by their gunners. As with the combat in the morning Park had great hopes in the Duxford Wing now over London. The great mass of British fighters were able to attack unescorted German bombers because their escorting cover of Bf109s had begun the return to base having run low on fuel and ammunition. There was carnage among the Dornier 17s with, for instance in the case of the flight from Antwerp-Deurne, less than half returned without combat damage. The key element in what was taking place on this day was the psychological one, with British airmen surprising the Germans with their fighting endurance and courage. Park's tactics of seeking to intercept the enemy constantly with pairs of squadrons had been shown to work. Success was not simply due to the numbers of aircraft launched – because more had been scrambled on previous days – but due to the quality of Fighter Command's performance.

This was an impressive day for Fighter Command, although in retrospect not as impressive as it first appeared. A tally of 183 German aircraft destroyed was reduced to 56 on closer scrutiny. But it could not be denied that this was the highest loss of aircraft in a single day suffered by Göring. Very disturbing for Park was the loss of thirteen of his pilots. For the first time, the RAF had enjoyed superior numbers of aircraft to those of the Germans. Churchill, who had been at Uxbridge watching it all unfold, said, 'Sunday's action was the most brilliant and fruitful of any fought up to that day by the fighters of the Royal Air Forces…. We may await the decision of this air battle with sober but increasing confidence.'

With the invasion scare at its height Park claimed after the war that the Air Ministry issued him with an order to be prepared to destroy every airfield within 11 Group.

On 18 September Park sent out orders of the priorities that were to be adopted in the event of an attempted invasion. Naval forces and bases would have top priority and protection given to Allied ships in conflict with German vessels. Attacks would be directed at enemy vessels and barges carrying troops, landing craft and tanks. The protection of the airfields would be in the hands of the RAF Regiment and the army. Park refused to countenance any surrender of airfields and they were to be held 'at all cost'. As far as communication was concerned, this should remain in the hands of each Group, and if this broke down responsibility would devolve to sector commanders. In turn, if this failed senior officers should act on their own initiative. Park's view of a German invasion was that it would only last for seventy-two hours, but conditions for defending forces during this period would be grim indeed.

Towards the end of September there was a great increase in the number of fighters the Luftwaffe was employing. Park struggled to get an appreciation of the formations because of low cloud and the difficulties of locating the bombers within the attacking group. His reconnaissance patrols were failing to produce the level of accuracy necessary and Park was forced back to the expedient of wasting resources by employing patrols. Dowding optimistically thought that the threat to the South East had diminished and some of the RAF's resource of pilots and planes might be employed elsewhere. On the other hand, although 11 Group's losses had diminished, it was required to be on perpetual alert for invasion.

For Park, as always, there was a major concern with the health of the men he led and he instigated measures to use the opportunity for rest and recreation when bad weather prevented flying. Systems of billeting were introduced to encourage his pilots to get nights of undisturbed sleep.

On the afternoon of 24 September an incident occurred indicating that the challenge of integrating fighter and bomber activity was as difficult for the British as for the Germans. Blenheims from Bomber Command were sent out to attack German minesweepers operating in the Channel. There had been a request for fighter cover but this had produced only a single Anson. Evill, who investigated, found that Coastal Command said it was not prepared to take part in the operation. Although Park's reserves were much stretched, three squadrons duly arrived at the designated place at the right time. As with the organization of Luftwaffe attacks, fighters operating at low levels protecting slow moving bombers were proved to be particularly vulnerable.

The height at which the broader conflict was being fought had moved up to 25,000 feet by October and Park noted the new superiority of the Luftwaffe aircraft equipped with engine superchargers capable of maintaining greater power. Developmental work on the Spitfire and Hurricane had not produced an answer to this. The new challenge was for fighters capable of operating at 40,000 feet and 400 mph. He felt that both aircraft were too lightly armed and suggested two cannons and four machine guns. His pilots had faced severe cold in their cockpits which had the effect of paralysing parts of the body, and, because of this, were encumbered with thick bulky clothing inhibiting movement and speedy response to emergency.

Despite the scaling down of the invasion threat, the Luftwaffe continued their attacks, now going over a wider field to include aviation factories in Bristol and Southampton. These attacks necessitated RAF responses, such as on 23 September when both radar and observers failed to determine whether there were bombers present in the large enemy flights. Allied fighters discovered that they were fighting Bf109s with superchargers.

There was some progress in October when VHS R/T equipment was introduced. It widened the whole scope of communication opportunities with squadrons being able to operate on separate frequencies when on a particular operation or to work on a unified frequency when operating in pairs or bigger units. But on 5 November, Park was pointing out that the mixture of VHF and HF operating within his squadrons meant they would often take off without all aircraft in the squadron being able to communicate with each other.

With the growing evidence of success in the Battle of Britain, Park considered the possibility of switching from defence to attack. He noted the vulnerability of the Luftwaffe airfields in the period before sunset providing an opportunity for surprise attacks in north-west France. Although Dowding was against the idea, Douglas said he was in favour. So it was that two Spitfires on 20 December, shortly after Park had been replaced by Leigh-Mallory, attacked the German airfield at Le Touquet.

It became increasingly evident that the Blenheim was not suitable for night fighting and Park was promoting the use of the Bristol Beaufighter assisted by ground radar. Unfortunately as they manifested many teething problems they were not a viable alternative. Park began working on a generic approach to night fighting covering guns, balloons and searchlights as well as patrolling aircraft. Rather than dispatching Park to a training centre, Dr Orange suggests that he would have been the right person to organise an effective night defence strategy with unique aircraft, specialist aircrews, a different range of tactics and systems of organization and control.

Park copied to Beaverbrook's son Max, who was one of his squadron leaders, his report on Fighter Command's September and October operations. This highlighted the challenges of adapting to the additional height at which the battle was beginning to be fought. Beaverbrook expressed interest in being able to help in time for an anticipated Spring offensive. Unfortunately in sending his report out in this way he annoyed Dowding because it had been sent before its official submission. Park had indicated that he was taking up a more offensive response to German attacks saying, 'I hope by Spring to have additional squadrons and to make it really offensive, instead of struggling against superior numbers over home territories.'

Meanwhile Park's more mundane activity to improve the maintenance and support at 11 Group airfields continued. Park was assisted by the Duke of Kent who had a post supporting welfare for 11 Group. He submitted a report that deplored the absence of adequate facilities present in every base he visited. This must have produced a positive response because he wrote to Sinclair, the Air Minister's Secretary, thanking him for action that then had been taken to improve living conditions at fighter stations. Park expressed delight at discovering on landing at Biggin Hill a specialist team working on a works programme needed for the station. This coincided with his move from Fighter Command, and Park reports that the Duke appeared to have thereafter lost interest in his work with 11 Group.

Park's predecessor Leslie Gossage wrote to Park on 26 November following his departure: 'You leave behind you a record of achievement and have given the country an overwhelming sense of security during the hours of daylight and maybe, by night too, before long.' Park said in his reply: 'As the senior members of my Group Staff deserve the lion's share of the credit for our successes, I am taking the liberty of showing them your letter, because they have not much recognition apart from my own thanks at the end of each phase of the operations.' In Gossage's view, lack of recognition reflected the central position 11 Group occupied in the conduct of Britain's defence. Park disagreed, citing the reluctance of the Air Ministry to support his recommendations for awards for members of 11 Group.

Looking back, the importance of the events of Sunday 15 September as a turning point for the Battle of Britain must be recognised. Every squadron in 11 Group was in action together with fighters from Duxford Wing 12 Group. In addition a squadron from 10 Group was called upon to protect areas in the south-west. The challenge to ground crews was to get aircraft refuelled and rearmed between enemy sorties. On this day, under Churchill's eye at Uxbridge, Park drew on all his experience to cope with large fleets of Luftwaffe bombers and fighters. His squadrons had success in breaking up Luftwaffe flights over London and forcing them to jettison their bombs away from main targets. Unlike Bader and the advocates of Big Wing tactics led by Air Vice-Marshal Leigh-Mallory (of 12 Group) Park placed great priority on preventing Luftwaffe bombers reaching their targets, and not necessarily achieving large statistical kills against returning aircraft. A lapse on the part of Park in forgetting his wife's birthday on this epic day was forgiven by her with the statement, 'I need no bigger gift then a large bag of German aircraft.'

Leigh-Mallory's report on the action on 15 September highlights the role played by five squadrons taking off from Duxford before noon. Three Hurricane squadrons patrolled at 25,000 feet and two Spitfire squadrons were 2,000 feet above them. Thirty enemy bombers were located south of the Thames Estuary flying northwards with a protecting fighter cover of Bf109s. The squadron leaders saw 11 Group move into attack and hung back to avoid any risk of collision. As their Hurricanes moved in to attack the bombers the enemy fighters broke away and were seen to climb towards the south-east making no further attempt to protect their bombers. They then were observed trying to escape towards the west and the south. Not all managed to escape and some were shot down by the Spitfires. At the same time the

Hurricanes destroyed any of the bombers they could locate. Leigh-Mallory reports that a further patrol later on that day was far less successful. When Park reported to Dowding he criticized Leigh-Mallory's description in his report of 12 Group's performance as being exuberant.

Park had used the respite in attacks on his airfields to reduce the sorties he had ordered before the London attack from 4,667 to 2,159 between 7 and 15 September. The move away from attacks directed at the airfields provided his pilots time to recoup and recover in between being scrambled. Park was able now to establish an improved infrastructure in response to German attacks. It was no longer necessary for Park's commanders to order newly trained pilots joining their squadrons into immediate action. They could be given some training with experienced pilots before going into combat. On his visits during 7 and 15 September Park was able to see the improved morale at his sector airfields.

In contrast, experienced pilots within the Luftwaffe were becoming aware that after two months of attacks victory appeared no closer. Galland commented: 'Failure to achieve any notable success, constantly changing orders betraying a lack of purpose and constant misjudgement of the situation by the Command had the most demoralising effect on the fighter pilots, who are already overtaxed by physical and mental strain.'

On 5 October Evill wrote to Dowding about the relationship between 11 and 12 Groups: 'There is a fundamental difference of attitude between the two groups, which arises from differences of the condition under which they are fighting.... It seems to me that 11 Group's position is entirely reasonable except that they seem to ignore the value of utilising large formations when time permits. I have the impression that 11 Group's Squadrons have been to some extent affected by constant fighting against superior numbers.... It must be good for our Fighter Squadrons as a whole, and unhealthy for the Germans, for us to push in a 3 strong Wing on occasions and reverse the position. I feel Park should give more recognition to this fact and endeavour to organise things so that he can deliberately use the strength of 12 Group's Wing at an effective moment in dealing with a mass raid.'

On 9 October Leigh-Mallory wrote to Dowding seeking to answer Park's complaints about the lack of assistance he had received from 12 Group. He protested that he was willing to assist 11 Group but had received the request too late. He outlined his objectives in mounting his operations as being 'to endeavour to meet the Germans on favourable terms and so inflict heavy casualties on them while incurring few casualties ourselves and to raise the morale of our fighter squadrons, as I believe they have been severely

Air Chief Marshal Sir Charles Portal and Air Vice-Marshal Park talking to fighter pilots

prejudiced by the very heavy casualties which have been caused by enemy squadrons, owing to the frequency with which a small number of our own fighters have had to tackle overwhelmingly superior numbers of German aircraft.' On 10 October Park again wrote to Dowding pointing out that it was out of the question to call up Big Wings from 12 Group of three to five squadrons when the attacks arrived at such short notice. Park did say that big formations had worked when the Luftwaffe had circled over north-west France waiting for their fighter escort and thus giving ample warning.

So much of Park's defensive tactics depended on superior intelligence and in this he was aided by security lapses of the Luftwaffe. One of the most valuable of these for Park was the ignoring of security by German aircraft by broadcasting wireless telegraphy (W/T) and radio signals in plain language which revealed the direction and altitude of their aircraft together with their rendezvous for their flight back to France. It was not appreciated by German High Command but there had been a turn of the tide in the Battle in mid-September with the week of 7 September marking the first time Hurricane and Spitfire losses did not exceed the ability of the country's aircraft industry to replace them.

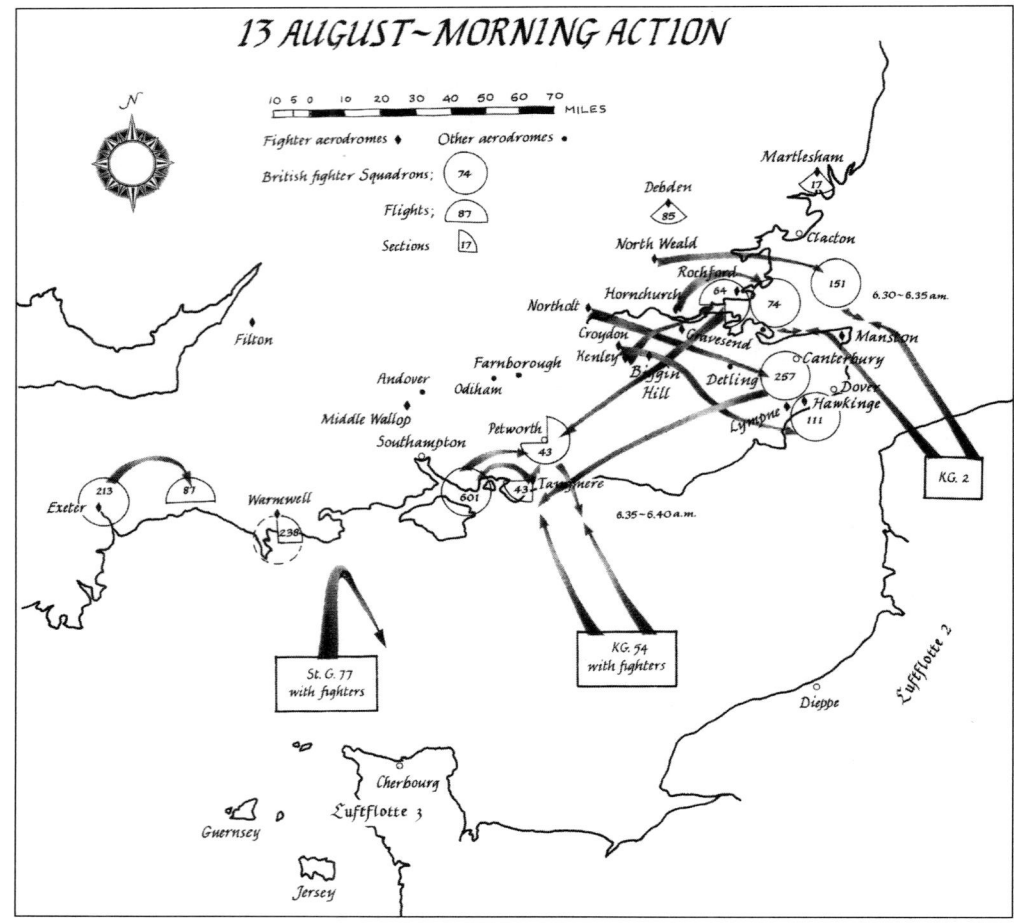

Pattern of fighting on 12 August 1940

With the Luftwaffe leaving his airfields alone Park was able to instigate a large programme of repair. He held back as many as possible of his fighters so that they could be called upon to attack Bf109s desperately low on fuel returning to France. Reinforced by two squadrons from Brand's 10 Group he tacked to the west over London so that he could meet the Luftwaffe head on. His fighters then began to attack German bombers and fighters as they returned to France short of fuel. He realised that the bombing of London created a basis for a reorganization involving moving some of his squadrons to sector airfields. He marvelled at the lack of innovation in the way the Luftwaffe were mounting their attacks, and looking at the plotting from his radar station at 16:20 hours on 9 September exclaimed, 'Same time, course, same target I would say.' Later he stated, 'The decision to bomb London was Germany's greatest mistake .... Our airfields were a shambles, pilot and aircraft strength were at an all-time low. By switching tactics and concentrating on London he will give us time to concentrate our forces.' Despite their opposition to Big Wing theory, when Dowding and Park judged the time was right they were not averse to ordering up a large flight, as they did over London on 7 September. Göring was now operating on a ratio of five fighters for each bomber to get his bombers through. At squadron level the war of attrition was taking its toll. For Park's pilots it was a desperate time. 'If you weren't in the air you were plastered,' Squadron Leader John Worrall says of this period.

The extent of the Germans' intelligence deficiencies is revealed by their belief that Allied losses were running at 800 Spitfires and Hurricanes out of an available frontline force of 915 and that Fighter Command were down to just 200 aircraft. In fact there were by now 750 serviceable aircraft flown by 1,381 pilots. In the third week of September the Chief Controller in the Air Ministry summed up the situation: 'I've been looking at the casualty figures and I have come to the conclusion that at our present rate of losses we can just afford it and I'm damned certain the Boche can't. If we hang on as we are doing I'm damned sure we shall win in the end.'

Alarm bells were beginning to ring on the German side. 'There is no sign of defeat of the enemy's air force over southern England in the crucial area where this is vital,' read an entry in the German Naval Staff Diary.

German pilots never saw an intelligence officer and had only casual information given to them by word of mouth. The extent of British losses was exaggerated. 'If German figures were correct they will be in London in a week,' Dowding commented. Park had been under pressure to commit a large number of squadrons in the face of overwhelming Luftwaffe numbers. He had replied, 'No one can be foolish enough to think that we can send any amount of fighters against large formations that the Luftwaffe are sending across the Channel and not receive casualties, but with careful placement of my squadrons it is hoped that we can keep them at bay.'

From coded inscriptions Park knew of the debate going on within German High Command about the date of a possible invasion, and on 15 September took steps to rearrange some of his squadrons with the defence of London in mind. This coincided with the arrival of Churchill at Uxbridge with his wife and private secretaries.

Park had to alter his tactics in response to these mass formations targeting London and he realised he had only about twenty minutes to scramble mostly Hurricanes, which were proving to have inferior capability to the Bf109s. Further, rather than continuing his policy of keeping aircraft on the ground until incoming enemy aircraft had been identified, on a launch-on-warning basis, he was forced to operate through standing patrols, which was fatiguing to his pilots, seriously affected his aircrafts' serviceability, and was wasteful of fuel.

Squadrons from other groups apart from 11 Group were expected to operate in a support role by protecting 11 Group airfields and providing a pool from which fresh squadrons could be drafted to replace those worn down by the intensive fighting found in the south-east. Park understood and operated on this basis but Leigh-Mallory did not. He had only a crude analysis related to the number of Luftwaffe aircraft shot down and turned a blind eye to the damage bombers could do if they were allowed to reach their destinations unchallenged. Leigh-Mallory demanded, with the support of Douglas Bader, that individual pilots should have licence to determine their own operational priorities. His was a challenge to the whole Dowding/Park operational system based on specific direction and the deployment of minimum aircraft. In truth what was taking place in the skies above Britain, which was totally different from the random dogfights in the First World War, was the background from which many senior staff in the Air Ministry defined their approach to the Battle of Britain. Fighter ace Johnnie Johnson from his own 12 Group observed that although Leigh-Mallory had no first-hand knowledge of fighter tactics he was still articulating his own views on the subject. His concept was of around sixty aircraft operating together as compared with the two squadrons operating separately of around twenty-four aircraft that Park advocated. Leigh-Mallory's concept was tactically naïve, ignored defence systems and was too cumbersome. It was said that when Leigh-Mallory's Big Wing arrived from their base in Duxford at Park's request all they saw was the tail fins of the departing German aircraft. Park complained that Leigh-Mallory's aircraft were rarely where they were required but popped up in places where controllers could not track them down and were fired at by Allied anti-aircraft guns. Dowding's comment on the Big Wing policy after the Battle of Britain was 'If the policy of big formations had been attempted at this time in 11 Group many more German bombers would have reached their targets.' Park added to this by saying, 'We would have lost the Battle of Britain if we had adopted the withholding tactics of 12 Group.'

Meanwhile Leigh-Mallory was pressing his case with an MP, Peter McDonald, an adjutant in Bader's squadron, and with the Under Secretary of State for Air Harold Balfour in favour of the Big Wing approach.

There was a human cost to all this. Sergeant J.H. (Ginger) Lacey, 501 Squadron Fighter Command: 'Towards the end of the Battle I had just taken as much as I could bear. My nerves were in ribbons and I was scared stiff that after one day I would pull out and avoid combat. That frightened me more than the Germans and I pleaded with my CO for a rest. He was sympathetic but quite adamant that until he got replacements I would have to carry on. I am glad now that he was unable to let me go. If I had been allowed to leave the squadron, feeling as I did, I am sure that I would never have flown again.'

On wing formations, Park's Order 20 of 28 September says: 'To counter enemy mass attacks, it has been hoped to develop patrol by wings of 3 fighter squadrons. Experience has shown, however, that even with a small amount of cloud squadrons take a long time to form up, and also have great difficulty in maintaining contact on patrol. Moreover the time taken to get 3 squadrons to a point seems to be double the time required for a pair of squadrons. With the RDF [Range and Direction Finding] giving us shorter warning than in the summer, we cannot afford to waste from 5 to 15 minutes while squadrons are assembling and sorting themselves out in wings of 3. Therefore unless the sky is clear of cloud layers and the Group controller gets ample warning of a heavy scale attack forming up over the French coast, he will dispatch pairs of fighter squadrons as described in instructions to Controllers No 16 during the winter months. This does not mean that wings of 3 squadrons will not be required on occasion in the winter, and frequently in the coming spring, when it is hoped we will be able to take a more offensive role and attack the enemy before he reaches the Kentish coast.'

Despite Park's reaction to Göring's switch to focus his attack away from 11 Group airfields, seeing it as salvation from possible defeat, some historians suggest that rather than Hitler's fateful decision to order the switch, it was the arrival of autumnal weather which provided a reprieve. A fundamental question is whether the Germans would have inevitably won without a switch in target or relief provided by deteriorating weather. Looking at the period from 1 to 18 September, a case can be made that finding glib explanations for Fighter Command's victory denigrates the valour of the few who achieved it.

Park's base at Uxbridge was not without its near misses. On 26 September a delayed action landmine landed between the police school and the WAAF quarters. It was not defused till the following day. On 28 September a bomb fell into a tree just fifty yards from the Operation Room and was taken away to be defused. On 6 October a Junkers 88 attacked the base and a bomb landed in the NAAFI shop damaging water and gas mains but causing no casualties.

Chapter 17

The Big Wing controversy

The Luftwaffe's reaction to the high level of losses it had sustained in recent weeks was to switch to night raids on London and bombing at high altitude. On 15 October there was an attack by 400 bombers. Based on Enigma encryptions and observation of barges leaving Channel ports, Churchill and Fighter Command decided that the invasion had been postponed. On 31 October Fighter Command had 729 fighters ready for action and 370 in reserve with another 110 being built at Southampton and Birmingham. From 31 July to

Members of the Air Council shown in 1941 who were responsible for the dismissal of Park and Dowding. Captain Harold Balfour, Under Secretary of State for Air; Sir Archibald Sinclair, Secretary of State for Air; and Air Chief Marshal Portal.

October 23rd, 1956.

Flight Lieutenant J. L. Hunt, OBE
Air Ministry,
Adastral House,
LONDON, W.C.1,
England.

My Dear Hunt,

Thank you very much for your letter of October 10th, and for the Press Cutting about the book written by Group Captain Johnson.

You said that many ex 11 Group chaps have wondered why I have not written my own account of the Battle of Britain. For your personal information, my reply is that I do not wish to hurt the friends and relatives of some very high-ranking officers still very much alive.

During the Battle of Britain there were two Air Marshals at Air Ministry who very much wanted Lord Dowding's job at H.Q. Fighter Command. At the same time Dowding was very unpopular with the C.A.S., Newall, who was very friendly with the aspiring Air Marshals at Air Ministry. Dowding was so highly thought of by the Cabinet that his position appeared to be unassailable, until the conspirators at Air Ministry discovered an Air Vice Marshal in No. 12 Group who badly wanted my job commanding 11 Group. Consequently, in October, when the Battle had been won, it was brought to the attention of the Air Secretary that Air Vice Marshal Leigh Mallory claimed that the tactical handling of 11 Group Fighters had been faulty, and that the mass formation tactics of his Group would have been more successful. The trouble was that neither Dowding nor I took seriously this criticism of my fighter tactics, because we were so confident that we had been right in the method of winning the Battle.

Imagine the surprise and anger of Dowding when, in October, 1940, he was summoned to attend an Air Council Meeting with me, to justify my fighter tactics in the face of critics from 12 Group. This Meeting was arranged without the knowledge or approval of Dowding, and I was asked to explain to the Meeting the reasons for my fighter tactics. As will be seen from the Official History of the R.A.F, this criticism after the event was used by the retiring C.A.S. and his Air Marshals, as an excuse for getting rid of Dowding. Of course, being his First Lieutenant and his tactical commander throughout the Battle of Britain, I was banished to a Training Command. The result was that Air Marshal Sholto Douglas, from Air Ministry, replaced Dowding in November, 1940, and, shortly after, I was replaced by his close friend, Leigh Mallory from 12 Group, whose malicious criticism had been used by the ambitious Air Marshals at Air Ministry.

Should I pass on before I have had an opportunity of writing a book, then I give you full permission to publish this letter so that ex-11 Group Members will know why a small section of the Air Ministry listened to the criticism of 11 Fighter Group, after the Battle had been well and truly won.

With kind regards.

Yours sincerely,

Keith Park

Copy of Park's response of 23 October 1956 to Flight Lieutenant J.L. Hunt about his dismissal

31 October there were 2,927 pilots who made 2,698 claims of victories during the Battle of Britain. Of these 806 were made by aces (104 being recognised as such). This underlines the reality of fighter squadrons in conflict stated earlier that in each squadron only a small proportion of pilots, 3 or 4, would achieve significant kills of the invading Luftwaffe. The total number of Luftwaffe pilots killed and wounded was 2,698 and for Fighter Command 544 lost their lives.

The Luftwaffe during September and October began to fit their Bf109s and Bf110s with a 25 kg bomb which was evidence of frustration in the German High Command at the vulnerability of German bombers. This change of tactic caught British observers by surprise as when reports came that London was being bombed they had only seen Bf109s. Park had heard this and his commanders were responding that what they could see were not bombers but fighters. This response is surprising because reports had been in existence since 9 September that the Germans were fitting bombs to their Bf109s. In practice Park found that his squadron commanders became quickly aware which of the attacking Bf109s were carrying bombs as these fighters had to fly at a lower level. This lack of height enabled 603 Squadron to sneak up on the first fighter bombing mission of the Luftwaffe and shoot four of them down. The fighter squadrons of the Luftwaffe had become demoralised at their high rate of losses. There seems little doubt that 12 Group made little or no contribution towards this. During October, squadrons from Duxford Base for instance flew fifteen sorties without making contact with the enemy.

Park was increasingly having to cope with fatigue among his pilots. On 1 November the loss of the highly experienced Squadron Leader Archie McKellar from 605 Squadron is a case in point. He disregarded an instruction to return to base when he had dived on enemy aircraft and overshot them. He appeared to forget that Bf109s operated in pairs and simply concentrated on one of a pair. But Park would note that despite the loss of McKellar the squadron maintained a high and increasing morale over the coming months.

On 11 November Italian aircraft were introduced to the attack on Britain, but mainly due to inferior aircraft the conflict was a disaster for them. Although Park received optimistic estimates much higher, the Italians actually lost three bombers and three fighters.

Park and the RAF had waged a relentless struggle in the face of a better-resourced enemy recognised as being the best air force in the world. Park's victory cannot be attributed to either radar or Luftwaffe mistakes. The victory's real origins lay in the fighting spirit of the RAF's pilots, and the quality of its senior leadership embodied in Keith Park.

It was Park who organised the great proportion of the battles and (although he made the mistake of using some airfields close to the south coast which were particularly vulnerable) provided the vision and leadership which was the key factor in victory. Simply seeing the Battle of Britain in terms of victories and losses as Göring sought to do does not provide an accurate picture of what took place. Christopher Bergström identifies 1,411 German losses while Fighter Command lost 1,135.

Throughout the Battle of Britain Park issued 31 Group Instructions, the last being on 17 October. These confirm that his responses to the changing course of the Battle were almost always correct. If a less perceptive man had been in command the Battle could easily have been lost.

One of the distinctive aspects of this part of the Battle of Britain was how a tussle for height developed between the combatants. Air fighting was taking place at higher altitudes. Park ordered, 'When time permits allow the planes to climb to high altitudes – Spitfires 30,000-35,000 feet and Hurricane Squadrons which have operated in pairs 25,000-30,000 feet before they are sent against German fighter formations.' As well as this he had a scouting unit formed, the 421 flight, with a role to patrol along the south coast to spot incoming Luftwaffe formations – a very dangerous and vulnerable mission for the pilots concerned.

In a paper to the Royal Air Force Historical Society on 25 June 1990, Vincent Orange sought to define what the essential characteristics for a commander might be. The first point he makes is that the Germans called Park 'Defender of London', but referred to Leigh-Mallory as 'The Flying Sergeant'.

The second point is the possession of crucial knowledge, and Orange points out that Park had been examining defence systems from as early as 1926/7 and he always maintained that Fighter Command had been in existence since 1936 before it formally came into existence.

In this period he had been a confidant of Dowding, which was recognised in 1938 when he became senior staff officer at Bentley Priory. His appointment by Dowding to take charge of the crucial 11 Group was not done on the spur of the moment but rather was based on a relationship of respect between the two men.

As any chronology of the day-to-day events of the Battle of Britain reveals, Park possessed the ability to articulate his ideas and listen to those of others. He could turn his observations about what was happening on the frontline into accessible language accommodating what he had been told. There can be no doubt that he possessed a ruthless streak, and here there is a contrast

Douglas Bader, whom Leigh-Mallory brought to 'The Meeting of Shame' of senior officers designed to undermine Park and Dowding

with Dowding who appears to have been more easygoing about the fissures in Fighter Command. Orange suggests a strange reversal of role, with Park manifesting Teutonic characteristics demanding order and systems while Göring revealed typically British traits such as a refusal to plan, dabbling with one expedient after another, and relying on appeals to honour and loyalty to compensate for technical and administrative failures.

A fifth point relates to Park's relationship with his sector commanders, where he expected and got more than routine agreement to his orders and instructions.

Orange highlights a sixth element at work: luck. In May 1938 Park had been dispatched to Palestine by the Air Ministry but because of illness was unable to take up his post. Arthur Harris's newly married wife was keen to see the Holy Land and a swap was arranged with Park taking over his role with

Fighter Command. Under Harris, 11 Group would have been commanded in a very different way.

The seventh point relates to events after Dunkirk and an understanding of the strategy required to hold out until the winter arrived and the country had been able to rebuild its defences. Against Park and Dowding was the loss of so many experienced and well trained pilots in the Battle for France and the fact that they had to be replaced by newly trained novices put up against battle-hardened Luftwaffe pilots whose experience went back to Spain in 1936.

The final eighth point is that the campaign was successful and the Battle had been won so it justified itself even if a large section of the Air Ministry disagreed with the tactics Dowding and Park adopted.

Essentially Sholto Douglas and Leigh-Mallory were completely wedded to the concept of flying in large formations. Park believed this was alien to defensive fighting, his reasons being the length of time it took for planes to form up after they were airborne, genuine difficulties of communication by squadron commanders or controllers on the ground, and the loss of the element of surprise because groupings such as this were easily spotted. A further reason was the limitation of the fuel supplies available, which affected both the Luftwaffe and RAF but in different ways. Park's complaint about this in relation to Big Wing was that the fuel used in forming up in large formations was not available to be used in conflict. Park realised that the Germans liked having the bulk of Fighter Command in one location because it enabled their bombers to proceed to their target unscathed.

At the root of this disagreement must be the proposition that Douglas and Leigh-Mallory were prepared to accept that the Luftwaffe could attack its targets without necessarily being engaged by the RAF's fighters but that the subsequent attacks on retreating bombers would bring a major return. This fails to recognise that attacks on 11 Group airfields and radar stations largely unopposed would have led to the collapse of the air defence system, the loss of early warning, and eventual failure.

The fighter ace Ginger Lacey characterized Big Wing as 'a cumbersome and time-wasting' method of getting aircraft to the killing ground, and 'if you did not get to the enemy bombers before they bombed, you are only doing half your job.' There is a real question why men like Sinclair and Balfour, who would decide the future of Dowding and Park, sought the views of Douglas Bader but not those of Ginger Lacey and Alan Deere.

Chapter 18

Meeting of Shame

Only in 1968 did Dowding publicly recognise the difficulties Park had experienced in 1940 from the animosity of Leigh–Mallory. 'I had no idea,' Dowding was reported as saying. 'What a wretched position to place Park in. I know now that he had tried to fight it out for himself and he deserves praise for that. But I might have been able to help him more. When the time came for me to intervene it was too late…. too late for both of us.' This is a strange comment because Park had drawn attention to Leigh–Mallory's mistakes and failings on a number of occasions.

Douglas Bader shared Leigh–Mallory's frustration at not being in the front line of battle. It was his view that it did not matter whether the invading bomber was shot down before or after it had dropped its bombs. He was supported by Sholto Douglas, a leading figure in the Air Ministry, who also believed defence of the targets under attack should be left to ground defence and attacks on the enemy could take place after bombing. Although Bader's claims of victories were regarded with scepticism by the Air Ministry, Leigh–Mallory continued to support them. Park scribbled a note on his copy of Leigh–Mallory's report: 'Did these wings engage before targets were bombed?'

The relationship between Park and Brand was what should have existed between Park and Leigh–Mallory. When it appeared that there would be heavy Luftwaffe attacks in the 10 Group area, particularly on aircraft factories, Park was speedy in organising assistance and Brand agreed with Park on an overall strategy.

Within the Air Ministry, work was being done to produce a critique of Park's tactics. Using Leigh–Mallory's original report supporting the operation of Big Wing configurations, they were critical of the way Park was operating in a way that his squadrons always met the enemy on unequal terms, both in numbers and height. Further, the operation of his squadrons was not properly coordinated and squadron leaders were not being given sufficient time to discuss or coordinate operations. It was claimed that squadrons were often instructed to patrol too low and to attack the enemy from below. Stevenson put forward the recommendation that the minimum number of squadrons employed should be three. Finally there was the announcement that on 17 October the Chief of the Air Staff would convene a meeting to discuss tactics employed by fighter aircraft and to hear a report on progress towards improvement in night interception. Those invited would include Dowding, Park, Leigh-Mallory and Brand. Stevenson circulated a report highlighting Leigh-Mallory's claims to have destroyed 105 enemy aircraft at a cost of 14 of his fighters. Before the meeting Park made a request that his two recent instructions covering five months of 11 Group experience should be distributed. The difference in his paper to that of Leigh-Mallory's was that his objective was the protection of aircraft factories and London and sector aerodromes, and not claims about enemy aircraft that might be destroyed.

Only twelve men plus two secretaries attended the meeting on 17 October. Because Newall was ill Douglas chaired the meeting. The attendees were Air Marshal Sir Charles Portal, Air Marshal Philip Joubert de la Ferté,

---

A Meeting held in the Air Council Room
on October 17th-1940 to discuss Major Day Tactics
in the Fighter Force

(Reference Air Staff Notes and Agenda Dated 14.10.40)

Present:

Air Vice-Marshal W. S. Douglas.	D.C.A.S.
Air Chief Marshal Sir Hugh C.T. Dowding	A.O.C.-in-C. Fighter Command
Air Marshal Sir Charles F.A. Portal	C.A.S. (Designate)
Air Marshal Sir Philip P.B. Joubert de la Ferte	A.C.A.S. (R)
Air Vice-Marshal K.R. Park	A.O.C. No. 11 Group
Air Vice-Marshal Sir C.J.Q. Brand	A.O.C. No. 10 Group
Air Vice-Marshal T.L. Leigh-Mallory	A.O.C. No. 12 Group
Air Commodore J. C. Slessor	D. of Plans
Air Commodore D.F. Stevenson	D.H.O. (Home Operations)
Air Commodore O.G.W.G. Lywood	P.D.D. of Signals
Group Captain H.G. Crowe	A.D.A.T.
Squadron Leader D.R.S. Bader	O.C. 242 Squadron
Wing Commander T.N. McEvoy}	Secretaries
Mr J.S. Orme}	

Fateful meeting of 17 October 1940.

Air Vice-Marshal Douglas Evill (not listed at the meeting on 17 October 1940), Air Commodore D.F. Stevenson, Air Vice-Marshal O.G.W.G. Lywood, Air Commodore Slessor, Air Vice-Marshal Quintin Brand from 10 Group, Air Vice-Marshal Leigh-Mallory, J.S. Orme (Secretary), Group Captain H.G. Crowe and Air Marshal Sholto Douglas. Against standing procedures Leigh-Mallory brought along with him Douglas Bader, a very junior officer within the RAF hierarchy. For balance, another pilot offering frontline experience should have been invited, but discourteously neither Park nor Brand had received any prior indication that this might be necessary. The net result was that Douglas and Leigh-Mallory could claim that Big Wing represented a progressive way forward by aircraft from Fighter Command. Douglas set out his agenda in the form of three propositions. Firstly when the invading Luftwaffe was encountered they should be outnumbered. Secondly they should enter any battle with a clear plan of action enabling a separation of the attack on the fighter escort and bombers. Finally there should be greater effort to secure a height advantage. Douglas in a long speech gave no indication that he had read and absorbed Park's reports or the many instructions he had issued.

Some in the room commented that Park seemed tired, which is not surprising considering the weight of responsibility on him over the last two years. Despite this he was still able to make a whole range of cogent points. It was however clear that there were a number in the room whose minds were already made up. Only when he retired did John Slessor speak out against what he called an unnecessary meeting in which there were a number of men largely concerned about their own advancement. Portal, with no experience of fighter policy, opted to support the opinions of Douglas and the group around him. Was there an element of class distinction at play? Douglas, Leigh-Mallory and Portal were all educated at British public schools in contrast to Park; being urbane and at home in society they were a different mould to the straight talking New Zealander. Moreover, Park was Dowding's man, deliberately selected over Leigh-Mallory, and if at last Dowding was to go, Park would have to go with him. A balanced view should have recognised the complexities of air defence which could not be explained in the simplistic terms presented by Leigh-Mallory. His suggestion that his aircraft operating to the rear of Park's could be in position to confront the invading Luftwaffe while Park's planes pursued the departing Germans was simplistic in the extreme. The radar available was primitive and could not distinguish accurately the height and volume of the approaching aircraft. Park knew that the approaching German aircraft were not aiming for a single target, nor would they fly in a straight line. There was no evidence that Leigh-Mallory's tactics of promoting fighter to fighter combat would have succeeded because for the greater part of the Battle of Britain fighters sent to confront the Luftwaffe were outnumbered. In fact in the critical stages the Luftwaffe had achieved a numerical superiority and British losses were 1,023 to German losses of 873.

The conclusions of the meeting recorded in its minutes were: 'The employment of a mass of fighters had real advantages, though it was not necessarily the complete solution to the problem of interception … and that it would be arranged for 12 Group to participate freely in suitable operations over 11 Group area.' Park followed this suggestion asking that a Wing be placed on permanent patrol for a definite time during the day. Leigh-Mallory rejected this idea. Dowding attempted a reconciliation by saying, 'as a result of recent discussions… 11 Group must always give 12 Group the maximum possible notice of a possible intention to call for assistance.'

On 21 October on receipt of the draft minutes of the meeting he regarded as containing 'misinformed criticism', Park sent a number of amendments requesting that they be included in the report of the meeting. He said, 'I cannot agree to the important statement which I made being omitted.' He criticized Stevenson's minutes of the meeting on the grounds that they recorded inaccurate information. Park emphasised that two squadrons were frequently scrambled, and that he had excellent coordination with 10 Group with regular conferences taking place for coordination. It would be impossible for 11 Group to operate Big Wing given his time constraints and its inherent inflexibility. Despite these protests Douglas and Stevenson were determined to show that Park had mishandled the Battle and rejected his amendments because of their length. Brand joined the argument on Park's side and wrote to Stevenson supporting his viewpoint only to see his view, like Park's, rejected by Douglas.

Minutes of the meeting state that an increase in the use of mass fighter formations had great advantages. It advocated 12 Group participating more freely in action over 11 Group's area. Leigh-Mallory followed this up by demanding that 12 Group be given more warning of any request for support in 11 Group's area. Rebuttal of this can be seen in Park's letter to Evill of 25 October complaining that although 12 Group had offered support they had returned from the Dover area after failing to make any contact with the enemy. On the 26th he wrote again to Evill about another failure to make any contact with the Luftwaffe due to delays in forming up the Wing.

Leigh-Mallory had responded by offering a Wing to counter enemy activity in the Dover Straits, but that was unsuccessful because of a failure in radio communication, and because his formation thought their participation was unnecessary as two of Park's own squadrons were seen above them. Park was also critical of the way 12 Group had employed the Polish Squadron, lacking he said the knowledge of the fighter tactics which should be employed. He attributed the failure of the Polish Squadron to operate effectively to a preoccupation with retaining a mass formation and not concentrating on locating and attacking the enemy. Following another complaint to Dowding about yet another failure by 12 Group to respond to a request for assistance, Dowding appeared to lose patience with Park: 'I think the answer is that 12 Group should not be called on for assistance unless and until 11 Group gets into difficulties owing to the number of its own squadrons it has had to use. It is absurd to call on 12 Group when only two 11 Group Squadrons have been dispatched.' On 13 November Dowding issued orders that 12 Group should hold two squadrons available for action at fifteen minutes notice, and action should be taken to improve communication.

On 29 October further evidence was provided that Big Wing tactics were not working. At 10.30 am the request to take action against incoming German aircraft was received by 12 Group. Leigh-Mallory's aircraft had left the ground by 10.47 am but had not left the Duxford area by 11.07 am. As a result they failed to intercept the approaching Luftwaffe. In the meantime Park responded to three more raids by scrambling eight squadrons to oppose them but with no assistance from the Duxford squadron because it was now landing having failed any interceptions. With seventeen squadrons airborne help was sought again from Duxford for them to patrol between Maidstone and Sheerness and then to intercept two raids crossing the Thames Estuary and heading for Essex. The instruction was ignored. Hornchurch could not get through to the Wing because of continuous RT traffic between the Wing and Duxford. When it was clear that the interception would be missed Leigh-Mallory was asked to have his Wing sweep north through north Kent to intercept other raiders. Instead he recalled it because of reports of deterioration in the weather at Duxford. His flight was grounded as an attack on East Anglian aerodromes was beginning.

Lawson, Evill's Chief Assistant, commented about what had happened. In the morning the Wing had been too slow in assembling over Duxford and height should have been gained while flying. There could be no criticism of not having been called soon enough because the enemy was crossing the coast. The second instance showed the profound difficulty of the flight to be effectively controlled when it was operating in the south. Park had to arrange for 11 Group fighters to accompany it while it was in the area working on an RT frequency to ensure that the flight could be plotted on the operating tables. Not only had the Wing failed to carry out the interception of 29 October, but it was not available when required to act in its own area to repel attack. The attack on the East Anglian airfields had been planned in such a way as to exploit the big raid in Kent and had found Leigh-Mallory without reserves.

The rift between Park and Leigh-Mallory remained. Douglas retained his dislike of Park and attributed the problem to Park's opposition to another group being involved in his area. Harold Balfour, Under Secretary of State, underlined Sinclair's findings in his report that 12 Group had experienced no contact with the enemy since September; he claimed that Park was jealous of 12 Group's ability to shoot down aircraft. Despite moves for 12 Group to support 11 Group this did not appear to be happening. Bader continued his stirring of the pot.

Dowding passed Balfour's report to Evill and asked for his observations. In Balfour's view there were four issues. The first was that 12 Group was not given access to all available radar information. The second related to Duxford's denial of the information provided by the Observer Corps. There was the familiar criticism that Duxford was not asked to help until it was too late. Finally there had been opportunities to destroy German aircraft that had been missed.

Evill commented on each of these points in turn. Firstly on the details of radar information, he had himself given orders about passing on initial radar plots. Secondly the practice of the Observer Corps at Bromley passing on radar information directly to Duxford had been stopped by the Southern Area Commandant of the Observer Corps and not by Park because of the difficulty of handing over tracks of planes between one observer area and another. On the third point, the Wing had in fact been called out too quickly without need on 29 October and the same thing had happened on 5 November. Finally 12 Group Big Wing absorbed the energies of four or five squadrons who had to be kept at readiness for a possible attack. Evill further criticized it for devoting too much time to forming up.

Somewhat exasperated, Dowding now indicated that he intended to monitor the operation of both groups from Bentley Priory. He believed that Balfour's conclusions were wrong and that a great deal of ill feeling in this controversy had been caused by Bader, who suffered from 'the over-development of a critical faculty'. He was protected from disciplinary action by his amazing gallantry.

The argument between Park and Leigh-Mallory became academic on 7 December when Leigh-Mallory was appointed to replace Keith Park. Before this on 17 November Portal had written to Sholto Douglas saying that he would take over from Dowding as Commander in Chief of Fighter Command. Dowding was to be retired. The argument against charges that this was a conspiracy within the Air Ministry was that Dowding had continued in post after his retirement date, being the only one with a detailed knowledge of how the system he had created operated. Moreover, that he was wearied by the strain of months of intensive activity and this was reflected in the conference of 7 September when he appeared to be willing to entertain defeat by the Germans, which could be interpreted as a lack of will to achieve victory. Thirdly Dowding had failed conspicuously to resolve the argument between Park and Leigh-Mallory. Finally it was felt that it was time to move towards an offensive policy now the defence of Britain had been achieved.

Leigh-Mallory took the opportunity to suggest that the Big Wing concept was now accepted policy. Douglas, the soon to be new Fighter Command commander, replied, 'I am very much in sympathy with the AOC 12 Group proposals. I am convinced we must try and get larger formations of fighters against the enemy mass formations… we must give the AOC 12 Group's proposals every possible support.'

Churchill had been under political pressure to sack Dowding. It originated from a letter from the 1922 Conservative Monday Club signed by Sir Reginald Clarry MP, its Chairman: 'The executive committee were requested to meet and hear certain criticisms of the Fighter Command (RAF) brought forward by several members. This meeting was held and I was requested to represent to you the lack of confidence in which Sir Hugh Dowding is held in certain quarters of the personnel of the Force, and of the grave concern felt by my executive.' Churchill's response was to rebuke Clarry saying that he believed it was inappropriate for parliamentarians to take such an active role in defining how well the leadership of the armed forces were performing. His displeasure went as far as suggesting that cabinet ministers should not in the future speak to Party Committees like the 1922 Club.

On 15 November Dowding forwarded to the Air Ministry Park's report on the raids in September and October. Park had criticized the delays occasioned by the use of Big Wings. In a covering letter Dowding stated it was only a satisfactory response to the German incursions if large groups of squadrons could be got up in the air to a strategic height in good time. He forwarded Park's report to Leigh-Mallory and sought his comments on the employment of Big Wings during October. This revealed that in ten operations based on Sheerness an average of 24 minutes had been spent on patrol and resulted in the destruction of just one Luftwaffe fighter. On the question of activity in bad weather 11 Group were operating under pressure while 12 Group were grounded.

Park had the major responsibility to ensure that the front line of resistance to Luftwaffe raids was adequately maintained through a continuous flow of aircraft. It was a positive feature that the Germans complained about how elusive British aircraft were. As Alan Deere had observed, maintaining a presence using large groupings of planes would have been a dangerous option.

The consequence of allowing the Luftwaffe to destroy 11 Group's sectors would have been to preside over the elimination of the group's communication system. Even the temporary loss of effective operation at bases like Biggin Hill during August had threatened ultimate defeat. German tactics were to lure Park into mass engagement and to exploit their superior numbers to attack elsewhere. Park successfully played for time knowing that the onset of winter would make invasion unlikely, that it would provide him with time to regroup, and it would give the army time to recover after Dunkirk. However, as late after the war as 1956 Douglas was still seeking to justify large scale action against the Luftwaffe as the most effective means of defence.

On 25 November 1940 Park was told that he would be relieved of his command. Park received a message from Richard Saul expressing regret at the decision. 'In view of the magnificent achievement of your Group in the last 6 months who have borne the brunt of the war they have undoubtedly saved England. My sympathy is entirely with you.' In reply Park said that his real disquiet was that Leigh-Mallory would replace him. 'In view of what little support 11 Group has had from 12 Group ever since way back in May the news has come as a shock. Your Group and 10 Group have always sent properly trained squadrons to relieve war-weary squadrons from the front line. Moreover your Group always co-operated in helping out with junior leaders and providing properly trained pilots required to replace wastage. On the other hand a number of the pilots provided from 12 Group were rejected by squadrons because they had not been trained before leaving the OTU.'

It was Park's objective view that if there were reasons for a change in the job it should have gone to Saul himself because he knew 11 Group's stations. 'What I have been told was the only reason for my leaving 11 Group was because I had carried the baby long enough for one man and was due for a rest from responsibility. I do not quite see why I should be stuffed into a busy office job at the Air Ministry.' He refused such a post and was then appointed to the Flight Training Unit.

When on 4 December Park was made a CB, Leslie Gossage sent his congratulations 'on an award which has seldom, if ever, been more richly deserved. The consequences of what you have achieved may prove well-nigh incalculable in the history of the world and my admiration for the way in which you have met and overcome the serious and novel problems which you have frequently encountered is unbounded.'

Park expressed his repeated wish that those who had provided him with excellent support should be acknowledged with awards as well. Wing Commander Victor Beamish, commanding officer of North Weald and a leading figure in 11 Group, wrote to Park expressing his regret at his departure: 'This feeling is reflected from all ranks, and we all wish to serve under you in the future,' he wrote.

Throughout 11 Group there was mystification and anger when news came that Park had in effect been sacked. This was exemplified by the commanding officer of Hornchurch Group Captain Cecil Bouchier who wrote about Park's original appointment and lasting support: 'We gained the one man above all in our Service who by his own infinite efforts and personal example would not only ensure ultimate victory but inspire it.'

Denis Richards, an official historian of the Battle of Britain, states, with perhaps some irony, that the transition of Park 'to quieter spheres… was not perhaps the most impressive immediate reward that might have been devised for the victors of one of the world's decisive battles'.

Park left the Command of 11 Group bitter about his demotion that, if allowed to dominate his behaviour, might have serious consequences for his future within Fighter Command. Late in 1941 he agonised over a letter he intended to send to Portal. He had come to believe that the reason for his removal from 11 Group was not because he needed a rest but rather that he had failed to cooperate with Leigh-Mallory. When his letter was finally dispatched he again pointed to the good cooperation with other group commanders but that 12 Group withheld cooperation in terms of relief squadrons and temporary reinforcement pilots. Park cited what Leigh-

Mallory had said at the meeting on 17 October 1940 that his Wings were effective against fighter raids, that they could be tracked and controlled by R/T south of the Thames, and that there was no delay in their arrival over the Thames at 25,000 feet within thirty minutes of Park making a request for their support. Park referred to records kept during the following weeks in October and November which found these claims to be incorrect. He did not wish to be reinstated to his old command, but 'I do however wish to clear my name of the damaging unofficial report that I refused to co-operate.' He summed up his vision for the future saying that he wished 'to command the biggest bomber group containing the biggest bombers carrying the biggest bomb to smash the Hun into final submission.'

Portal wrote back immediately, reiterating that he had been relieved of his command 'because we considered it unwise and unfair to allow you to continue to bear for another year the heavy strain which must fall on the AOC of 11 Group.' Portal urged Park to disregard idle gossip, and Park, pleased with the prompt reply, replied that his reply had taken a weight off his mind. Park said he was counting the days till he could have another crack at the Hun.

On the same day, 26 October, Dowding had written an article in the *Sunday Chronicle* in which he criticized the first official pamphlet on the Battle of Britain for the suggestion that the German attacks had been easily beaten off. He praised Park's initiative and resourcefulness in countering every tactical move by the Luftwaffe. 'I think I shall do you justice,' Dowding wrote to Park in a letter accompanying a copy of his *News Chronicle* article. Park wrote back saying that he had heard that Leigh-Mallory was still dwelling on the meeting of the previous year and joining with Sinclair in claiming that victory would have been achieved earlier if Big Wing tactics had been put into operation.

There was belated recognition of Park's abilities in January 1942 when he was moved from Flying Training Command and ordered to Egypt.

But the battle about Big Wing continued. Air Chief Marshal Sir Philip Joubert de la Ferté made the case for Big Wings in his book *The Fated Sky* and a following book *The Third Service* in which he praised Leigh-Mallory for 'a brilliant brain and his character was determined and cool'. Damning Park with faint praise, he said he was a good pilot but Leigh-Mallory could run rings around him. He said that Park suffered from a sensitive ego which did not help in his relations with other people. A group of people including his personal clerk at South Cerney came to Park's defence, including Lady Park who penned a reply in the London evening papers, and a former flight sergeant in the Signals Branch at Uxbridge resenting Joubert's criticism who said, 'As long as any members of 11 Group are still alive we will actively repulse any criticism of Park.'

Professor Ovary's comment is apt: 'Throughout the Battle a backstairs intrigue was conducted against Newall and Dowding involving among others the veteran airman Lord Trenchard and the Minister of Aircraft Production Lord Beaverbrook. A whispering campaign against Newall's alleged incompetence was begun by a junior officer in the Air Ministry and reached Secretary for State for Air Sinclair and also Churchill.'

As Marshal of the Royal Air Force Lord Tedder, one whose judgement surely speaks for itself, said about Park, 'If any man won the Battle of Britain he did. I don't think it is realised how much that one man with his leadership, his calm judgement, did so much to save, not only this country, but the world. To his fighter boys from Australia and New Zealand he listened to the blokes who were doing the job. He saw pilots after patrols that had seen their best friends go down in flames. He would have a cigarette with them, and was looked on in return as one of the boys.'

Historian Stephen Bungay comments: 'During the long months of the campaign Park hardly put a foot wrong, making all the major tactical decisions, attending to relevant details, visiting pilots and airfields himself and fighting internal political battles.'

Park: 'That is what I have never been able to understand. Everything went by the board: courtesy, good manners, the customary practices, the drill or procedure or whatever you like to call it. The whole way the thing was done was hole in the corner, just as if something had to be hushed up… so many times I have asked why this extraordinary situation was forced upon me.' He too later described his deep hurt: 'To my dying days I shall feel bitter at the base intrigue which was used to remove Dowding and myself as soon as we had won the battle.' Park was to nurse this anger for the rest of his life.

Dowding had held his position for four years; Park had only been in post for seven months and was a far younger man. Later in life when asked to reflect on his contribution to victory in 1940, Park's bitterness revealed itself. 'A great deal of personal satisfaction has long been destroyed by the scheming and deceit of envious senior officers in No. 12 Group and the Air Ministry after we had won the Battle of Britain,' he recalled.

Group Captain Peter Townsend, who would become famous after the war through his relationship with Princess Margaret, expressed a concern that Dowding's and Park's contribution to victory was not better known by the

British people: 'The two victors both realised the sad truth that men are seldom grateful for their saviours. But in this case the British people under heavy fire from the enemy could be forgiven for not knowing they owed their salvation to Dowding and Park, especially as both men had remained in the background throughout the battle.'

Churchill, who had only very reluctantly agreed to the dismissal of both men, wrote to Sinclair to voice his disapproval: 'The jealousies and cliquism which had led to the committing of this offence are a discredit to the Air Ministry, and I do not think any other Ministry would have been guilty of this piece of work. What would have been said if the Admiralty had told the tale of Trafalgar and left Nelson out of it?' One must wonder whether this cutting comment hit home with Douglas, Leigh-Mallory and Portal.

It is useful to consider the relative merits of Leigh-Mallory and Park as outlined by Sir Kenneth Porter: 'I served under Park and Leigh-Mallory. At first I thought Leigh-Mallory was useless, but he learnt very quickly. He later ran a paper exercise in the ops. room that failed and this converted me against Big Wing. He didn't however make decisions as quickly as Park. Park's conduct of the Battle of Britain was brilliant; he held a morning meeting and then flew around the airfields talking to the pilots, decisions were made by telephone (nobody used a file) and everything was done quickly. Everybody admired him but he was the most unlovable man. Leigh-Mallory on the other hand was a very nice man but relied very heavily on advice. Bader impressed him and took advice over Big Wing. Then at 11 Group he took advice elsewhere and picked people he thought knew what they were talking about and used them. Park never did this and he made enemies. He had no friends in the hierarchy, he was a loner. Leigh-Mallory was much more senior and got on well with other people including the Americans. He was not as pompous as some thought.'

The New Zealand ace A.C. Deere sums up his analysis of the Battle of Britain in this way: 'The Battle of Britain has gone down in history as a great victory, and it was due not so much to successful tactics as possession of an advanced air defence system backed by inspired team work and inspired leadership at all levels. Tactics were of course important to the outcome, in the finely balanced fighting towards the end of August they were perhaps all important, and perhaps the overriding factor that ensured final victory. Victory proved Park's tactics to be right in the particular circumstances, and however one might lean towards the Wing concept, it is difficult to envisage success other than in the way it was achieved, and combination of flexibility and economy of force.' He goes on to quote Basil Liddell Hart: 'The Germans bid to gain control of the air as a preliminary to invasion was frustrated by the superb effort of 50-odd squadrons of Fighter Command under the masterly direction of Air Chief Marshal Sir Hugh Dowding and Air Vice-Marshal Sir Keith Park.' Praise indeed from a master strategist.

Another insight into how Park was regarded by the men and women he led is provided by Sandy Johnson recorded in Laddie Lucas's book *Thanks for the Memory*. His squadron had been transferred from Scotland to the South to fight in the Battle of Britain. He was placed in charge of Spitfires operating out of Westhampnett in West Sussex arriving during the second week of August. Although he had been told that Park was a regular visitor to all his bases he did not meet him till 7 October. Unlike Park, the airmen he met had long since learned that it was vital to have camouflage dark clothing in the cockpit. Park appeared with his bright white helmet and immaculate white overall suit.

The atmosphere surrounding him was in striking contrast to the remote atmosphere that usually surrounded senior RAF officers. He clearly was someone with a clear remembrance of what it was like to be at the level of those he visited in the RAF hierarchy. He was characterized by good listening skills bolstered by the fact that he wanted to hear directly about the encounters with the enemy his airmen had experienced. He listened carefully to the grumbles that came forward while clearly separating the genuine complaints from the time wasters. Park would then draw his listeners into a communal group as he outlined the problems he was experiencing at headquarters level. This left the remarkable impression with his listeners that they were in the driving seat in the conduct of the war. Johnson felt that in his own way Park envied his pilots for being in the driving seat of the events of the war – a place he would like to occupy because of the kudos it brought. He claimed that he had been in contact with the enemy in his Hurricane, but this was never verified. Johnson identified Park's vanity, being something of a peacock, but felt in some unique way it was understandable.

Park resisted all attempts to persuade him to write about his experience. 'I have never felt strongly the need to produce a book to explain my actions in the Battle of Britain now that others have fully endorsed my fighter tactics,' he said. This is a statement that perhaps shows Dowding's weakness. Surely he should have gripped Leigh-Mallory and if necessary relieved him of his command? And did he show his support for Park at the time sufficiently strongly?

Dowding's salute to Park came later as well. 'If it hadn't been for Keith Park's conduct in the Battle and his loyalty to me as Commander in Chief we should not be here today,' he commented to Alan Deere in 1970. 'Leigh-Mallory should never have been allowed to take the line he did.'

Ahead of Park was the post of Air Officer Controller in Egypt and in 1942 a leading role in the defence of Malta. By February 1945 he was Air Controller of South East Asia. His war experience finished in 1946.

Chapter 19

Aftermath

Sholto Douglas and Leigh-Mallory's behaviour after the dismissal of Dowding and Park was shameful. Notice of each dismissal was carried out in a casual way and when reports were issued about victory in the Battle of Britain neither man was mentioned. Only belatedly was any effort made to rectify the situation, with Park being called to Buckingham Palace on 4 December 1940 to receive a CB.

Park received many letters of congratulation. His response was to take up his new position with enthusiasm. 'Maybe I shall be able to help Fighter Command by raising the standard of the FTS pupils we send to the OUT [Officer Unit Training]. To that end I wish one of your staff could write to me direct at No. 23 Flying Training Group and let me know where our weakness lies. I cannot promise an immediate cure for every fault, but I would like to know in what direction I can assist Fighter Command to defeat the enemy in 1941.' Park sent his own congratulation to Richard Saul who had replaced Leigh-Mallory at No 12 Group.

Sebastian Cox describes as a myth the idea that it was the manoeuvring of Sholto Douglas and Leigh-Mallory that brought down Dowding and Park. If this were so it ignores the authority possessed by more senior figures on the Air Staff such as Portal and Sir Wilfrid Freeman. Cox found it hard to believe that men like this would have agreed to the recommended dismissals coming from officers who were junior to them and clearly had career ambitions. Cox believed that Dowding's dismissal was related to his lack of action on the pressing problem of night bombing. Another major factor was Dowding's inability to take effective action about the growing rift between Park and Leigh-Mallory, two crucial group commanders. Clearly the fractured relationship between the two men had placed the efficiency of Fighter Command in jeopardy. Douglas had written to Dowding pointing this out and Cox makes the case that it should have never been necessary for a deputy chief of the Air Staff to write in this manner to his operational commander.

Denis Richards on the other hand defends Douglas against charges of being a schemer saying that he was a clever man but had uppermost in his mind the challenge of producing an effective night defence.

Leigh-Mallory never thought it necessary to have a formal handover at Uxbridge and made no contact with Park to facilitate his move to 11 Group. However, Park came to appreciate the brighter side of his new situation. Behind him in Uxbridge were scores of letters of appreciation from all levels within Fighter Command and even outside the RAF. For the next few months he still retained his position as a Group Commander. It was becoming obvious now that the war would continue for many months, and the key role he now was to occupy in training was recognised by people such as Balfour as being a crucial one. Park set about reorganising fighter pilot training in his usual diligent and dedicated way and had visited all the training centres he was responsible for by the end of January 1941.

By year end training schools in, for example, Canada had begun to produce a steady stream of pilots, so the urgent need for pilots to plug holes in Fighter Command's squadrons became less acute. There was another approach to give him a pen-pushing post within the Air Ministry which like the earlier one at the end of 1940 came to nothing.

Chapter 20

Egypt

On board the *Viceroy of India* taking Park to Egypt via Sierra Leone from where he would fly on, Dr Orange records an incident underlining Park's impatience with needless military authority. A young New Zealand pilot, John Mason, had been using a part of the deck reserved for officers and was ordered below by an officer. When told about it Park intervened and said they should share all facilities then available only to officer rank.

This was a period of Park's war when he would be separated almost permanently from his wife Dol and his children.

He was to take responsibility for the day and night fighter squadrons based in the Middle East. A system of collective defence was being developed, although it was always under-resourced bearing in mind the vast area involved. He was working under the command of General Sir Claude Auchinleck and was in post when the Allied defeat occurred at Tobruk.

Another New Zealander involved in Egypt was an outstanding airman and air tactician, Arthur Coningham, who worked at his side. Towards the end of his period in Cairo Park wrote: 'As I drove past I felt a little reflected glory in the fine achievement of the DAF [Desert Air Force] because my command had been able to give them such sound administrative backing as our army fell back in Egypt. I also reflected on what grand bombing targets those airfields offered to the Luftwaffe. Looking back over the war as a whole I believe that if the Luftwaffe had been able to obtain even temporary air superiority during the critical months from June to September 1942 our army would not have held Rommel at El Alamein.'

There are entries on 10 October 1942 in Park's diary about his frustration with the military hierarchy organising the campaign in the western desert. He refers to 'bad leadership, lack of discipline and a general debacle' which resulted in the destruction of hundreds of military vehicles and with them crucial supplies. He expressed concerns over the way Allied military transport was left isolated and forced to operate ahead of ground troops. His comment on the management of the campaign in Egypt was that it failed to reach the standard of a village cricket team. He could find little to be proud of. Park welcomed the arrival of Montgomery and the prospect of 'putting up a good show this time'. He reports he had 450 serviceable fighters against the Germans' thirty-five Bf109s.

Despite the positive aspects of his relationship with Churchill during the Battle of Britain, Park shows him to be a mixed blessing when he visited troops in action in the Middle East. Park shared a plane with him during his period in Egypt before taking over his command in Malta. He complained about Churchill's continual interference with its navigation, the way he spent a great deal of time interrogating the navigator, and the way he removed maps to study in detail the location of the aircraft. During the journey he continually interfered in the management of the war in Egypt. Park sums him up: 'Whatever his merits he has many disadvantages.'

Chapter 21

Malta

Air Vice-Marshal Hugh Lloyd, whom Park replaced as RAF Commander on Malta, had already stayed longer in post than planned when Park arrived to replace him on 8 July 1942. Malta was experiencing 117 days of bombing with as many as ten air raid warnings in a single day. Because of the shortage of pilots to replace those who had reached their maximum period of service on the island, there were fewer pilots than serviceable planes available. Lloyd was very much aware of how close the island had previously been to capitulation: 'A few bombs on Kalfrana air base during the previous summer would have ruined any hope of it operating as an airbase,' he had reported. There was a desperate shortage of spare parts and many of the Spitfires and Hurricanes were kept in operation by stripping aircraft that had crashed. As well as this Park would face a shortage of fuel, as had Lloyd, and had to maintain a sharp eye on any fuel wastage.

From May the air defence of the island had become more secure. Park was able to set about building up a bomber force which would enable him to go on the offensive. This would require rebuilding 69 Squadron which required the appointment of a competent, efficient commander. This he found in Adrian Warburton. He took over a squadron with a number of Baltimores and Spitfires. Fortunately the Pedestal Convoy was able to deliver ammunition for the attacks Park proposed on Rommel's supply lines to North Africa, and Park was able to create three flights within the same squadron mixing bombers and fighters. This was not without its organizational headaches.

Arriving with Park was Wing Commander J.M. Thompson DFC who had eight victories in the Battle of Britain and who on 14 July took over the Takali Wing on the island. Park lost no time signalling for supplies: fuel and spare parts. He set about issuing orders to maintain wireless discipline and not fire off ammunition at long distance targets. By 18 August Park was up in a Beaufort carrying out a survey of the searchlights around his airfields. He was also able to welcome fellow New Zealanders like Battle of Britain ace

Park at the controls of a Hurricane, Malta.

Colin Gray when he arrived on the island. Park drove him around the island in his red MG, impressing Gray with both his efficiency and his knowledge of the situation in the battle for Malta.

Lloyd, the man he was replacing, was not universally loved on Malta, possibly because he lacked Park's understanding of operational problems. In contrast Park had proved capable of mounting a defence against all odds. However, Lloyd had been the bastion defending the island coping with a manifest number of shortcomings in supply.

Park got off to a bad start, flying in on a Sunderland flying boat that had to circle the island which was then under attack. Lloyd reminded Park that he had taken Malta through its worst times when it lacked the aircraft to defend itself against almost continuous attack. He told Park, 'You see that Malta can take it.' Park noticed the sign outside Lloyd's office: 'Less depends on the size of the dog in the fight than the size of the fight in the dog.' Lloyd upbraided Park although he was junior in rank for the way he had risked his life flying in from Gibraltar in the middle of an attack when Lloyd had issued instructions not to attempt to land on the island. Lloyd's last two months in charge, April and May, had been particularly difficult, with attempts by convoys to reach the island being crushed by German and Italian aircraft. There is some dispute about the claim made by Park that he pioneered the tactic of meeting attacking aircraft ten miles away from the island to protect its airfields. An advantage Park enjoyed was that his arrival coincided with the sending of 30 more Spitfires, 29 of which arrived safely.

Park replied directly to Lloyd: 'I think you are dumb – why don't you stop the bombing and get on with the war instead of sitting back and taking it.' A message that was perhaps a bit hard; in fact he was fortunate that the *Eagle* and *Furious* between them were able to deliver to the island 125 Spitfires following the development of techniques enabling aircraft to take off from ships that were not carriers which came to fruition in the next few months. Although there was a high level of carnage among vessels in the Pedestal Convoy, the *Ohio*, a fuel tanker which had been hit, was towed into port providing desperately needed aviation fuel shortly after Park's arrival. Within a short period of time Park was able to operate with 100 aircraft, which outnumbered those available to the Axis. He was lucky!

The island's airfields were now being more effectively protected. Whether it was Lloyd or Park who developed the strategy of forward defence aimed at meeting attacking aircraft ten miles from the island's coast, there were now sufficient aircraft to implement this policy. As well as these having been forced to leave the island during the worst days of the siege, the bomber and torpedo squadrons were able to return. 'Our day fighter strength has during June and July been greatly increased and the enemy superiority in numbers has long since dwindled. The time had now arrived for our Spitfire squadrons to put an end to the bombing of our airfields by day. We have the best fighter aircraft in the world, and our Spitfire pilots will again show their comrades on the ground that they are the best fighter pilots in the world' (Park's special order of the day, August 1942).

On 23 July Park promulgated his interception scheme using the island's limited radar and radio contact resources. The downside of this was that any Allied pilot shot down would probably be drowned. In an attempt to limit these losses operating close to the island Park established a rescue boat which saved a number of lives. By 16 October Park was sending to his pilots a note of congratulations: 'Grand work, fighter boys. Your magnificence in the last few days is being watched not only in Malta but by the RAF on other fronts as well as by our Russian allies. Although heavily outnumbered last May, the Malta Spitfires came out on top and I am confident that you will win the second battle of Malta. Some of the enemy bombers have shown that they cannot take it. Keep it up and in the next few days the other German bombers will throw in the sponge. Replacement Spitfires and pilots are on their way but there is still some stiff fighting to finish. Good luck and good shooting. The work put in by maintenance personnel is much appreciated but the serviceability of our Spitfires continues to fall. You must get it up again. Where you have worked hard you must work harder and faster. Give our fighter boys Spitfires and we will drive the Hun out of the sky.'

As in 1940, Park was facing Kesselring who had been moved to command the Luftwaffe in the Mediterranean.

Despite a general ban on any non-urgent use of petrol Park insisted on driving around in his bright red MG. Even the general in charge, Gort, forsook his Rolls Royce in favour of a bicycle, but not Park. Because of the leading position of Fighter Command on the island there was frustration at the Union Club in Valletta about the way Park and the RAF had superseded officers from the army and navy. To the overwhelming majority Park could do no wrong and his visits to the bases and airfields were anticipated eagerly.

Invitations to meetings in his office at his headquarters in Valletta were a special event, always featuring a bottle of gin Park provided to get his guests talking in a free and uninhibited way. In this way he could learn first-hand about what he referred to as 'The sharp end'. While new uniforms and even laundry facilities were at a premium he managed always to appear immaculately dressed. Having visited all the airfields and bases on the island Park set about working towards using Malta as a base to attack Rommel's supply lines to Egypt. This involved fitting additional fuel tanks to increase the flying time of his aircraft and enable them to bomb and carry torpedoes. Park commented, 'The reason I introduced a fighter bomber was that the enemy was ignoring our fighter sweeps over his aerodromes in the south of Sicily. I used Hurricane bombers at first and the enemy reacted by sending up his fighters to intercept. As a result of flying trials we found that the fitting of two 250 lb bombs to the Spitfire slightly increased take-off run, and slowed the rate of climb by 10 per cent. There was practically no difference in speed involving level flight. We designed the bomb gear so that there was no loss in performance when bombs were being dropped. Unlike the Hurricane bomb gear, our Spitfire throws away all external fittings with the exception of a steel rib which protrudes less than one inch from the wing.' This reveals Park's firm grip on the technical practicalities of moving from securing Malta as a bastion of resistance to supporting the Allies' campaign in Italy.

Park's innovations were to play a crucial role in attacking Axis shipping moving from Western Greece to Italy.

There was still the reality of food shortages on the island with families being limited to half a loaf of bread each day. Eggs from neighbouring Gozo Island had to be reserved for hospitals.

On 20 October Axis bombers renewed an air offensive on the island. This was only partially effectively resisted by Park's Hurricanes and Spitfires meeting the enemy flights more than ten miles away from Malta – some bombers still managed to reach the island.

General Gort sent Park congratulations on this partial success. 'All ranks of the army send their heartiest congratulations to their comrades of the RAF on this magnificent achievement.' Park replied, 'All ranks of Malta RAF greatly appreciate your message of congratulations of the recent success of fighter defences. We are very grateful for the existence of our comrades in the army in keeping our aerodromes working at high pressure. The Spitfire squadrons are especially grateful for the helpful cooperation of anti-aircraft batteries in the engagement and breaking up of enemy formations that crossed

Ground crew, Malta.

Above and left: In the first photo Park is being driven visiting his air bases in Malta. In the second he is at the wheel of his red MG with Coningham.

Below: Ground crew with a Spitfire, Malta

Bases on Malta.

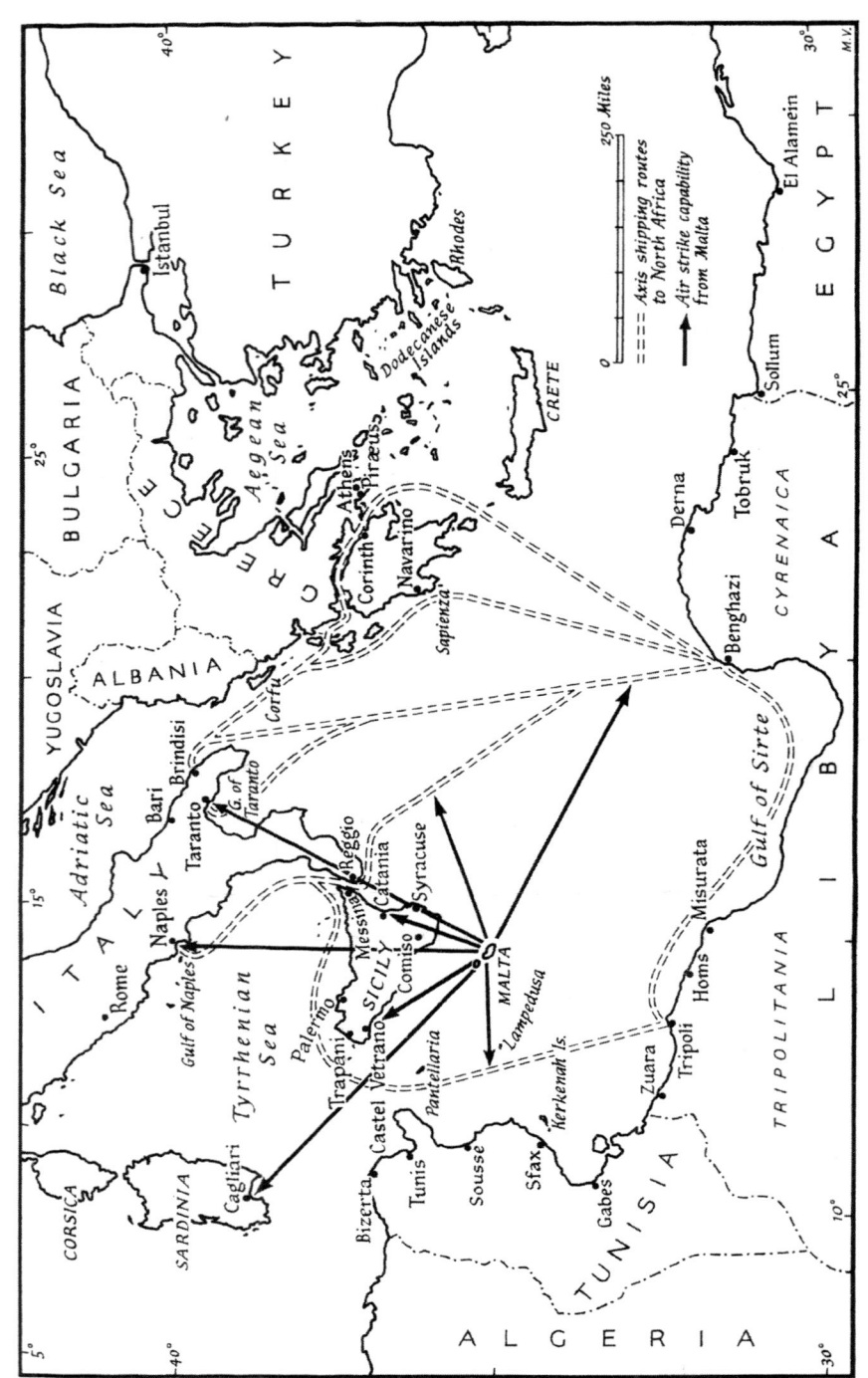

Now on the offensive from Malta – attacks on Rommel's supply routes.

Park meeting General Eisenhower.

New Zealand Pilots of 48 Squadron.

our coast. In spite of the enemy bombing of our aerodromes in recent days we have carried out more attacks on his shipping in the past 10 days.'

These public pronouncements did not disguise the internal conflicts occurring within the Malta High Command. Vice Admiral Power commented,

'Park is intensely insensitive – he doesn't understand the naval aspect and is very unsatisfactory to deal with.' A later comment: 'There is no depth in the man,' and later, 'Park is a conceited idiot …. a twister,' is evidence of exasperation of the island's administration with Park from Bonham-Carter the Governor on Malta. General Gort complained that Park was not showing the signals he was receiving from the War Office. The advice given to Park on 4 October from the Air Ministry was that he should show Gort 'too much rather than too little in the future'.

On the other hand there was a growing relationship between Park and General Eisenhower, Supreme Allied Commander, which was to develop as the war continued. Commenting on the way Park had moved from defence to attack, Eisenhower complimented Park, 'My admiration for your deeds past and present is exceeded only by my appreciation of your support.' News from Malta was providing the war effort with good news, and Portal and Freeman at the Air Ministry appreciated the positive comment appearing in the British and Commonwealth press.

But Vice Admiral Power remained critical, complaining again about how difficult Park was to work with. New American Mosquitos had arrived but the feeling was they were inferior to the Spitfire. Out of the fifteen new arrivals eight were quickly grounded due to lack of spares. Park attended a crucial conference in Algiers planning military action in North Africa which he described as being 'like Alice in Wonderland'.

Chapter 22

Now onto the Offensive

There were five fighter squadrons now on the island: 126, 185, 229, 249 and 1435. Park now for the first time had at his elbow 100 serviceable fighters. He could now protect Malta's airfields through his 'forward interception plan'. The German attempt to bomb Malta into submission in October had failed. Park now had the resources to attack Italian shipping supplying Axis troops in North Africa. He recognised that reconnaissance would be crucial and (reconnaissance) PRU Spitfires were employed for observation of the Italian fleet at Taranto, Messina and Naples, this being carried out often three times a day. Spitfires from Malta provided vital aerial cover for the Allied campaigns in North Africa. Park welcomed the arrival of the first aircraft with sufficient fuel to be able to fly directly from Gibraltar on 25 October.

Park at the controls of his aircraft.

One of the criticisms of Park made by Leigh–Mallory and Sholto Douglas was that he was not offensive enough in managing the operation of Fighter Command and that greater store should have been put on counter-attacks on Luftwaffe airfields in France in 1940. The fallacy of this argument was quickly revealed when Leigh–Mallory replaced Park and attempted to attack French airfields. The scale of his losses was greater than that which the Germans experienced in their attacks on Britain in 1940. When Park was asked to switch from defence of Malta to attacks on Axis lines of supply in the Mediterranean, his success in managing these attacks brought praise from Eisenhower and Montgomery as they were a factor in the Allies' success at El Alamein, Tunisia and Sicily.

Any belief that Park was immune from the danger his pilots lived with every day is undercut by an incident that occurred in January 1943. In transit to Cairo in a twin-engined Beaufighter he was attacked by five German bombers who destroyed one of his plane's engines when he was at least 150 miles from land. For placing himself at such risk he received a dressing-down from his old adversary Sholto Douglas when he finally reached his destination at High Command Headquarters in Cairo.

Park's last major defensive battle came after Rommel's final thrust at El Alamein. Based in Malta, Park's aircraft helped attack the supply lines of convoys supporting Axis campaigns in Tunisia. This involved up to fifteen operations per week. With the failure of Rommel's final offensive in August 1943, Park was tasked to produce a more comprehensive campaign with the eight squadrons he had at his disposal on Malta as part of a wider programme to disrupt Rommel's supply lines.

With victory at El Alamein, Park moved to organising support for the troops both in Tunisia and Sicily. On Malta, Park was involved in the construction of a combined war room with the army and naval forces in which General Alexander masterminded the invasion of Sicily. New airfields, radar installations and control rooms were also constructed. By the time of the invasion of Sicily there were forty squadrons operating from Malta, Gozo and Pantelleria.

Chapter 23

Park at the War's end

On 1 September 1943 Park was in London for discussions with Air Chief Marshal Sir Wilfrid Freeman about his future. There was debate within the Air Ministry about Park's virtues, but he at last became an Air Marshal. There was a discussion about replacing Cottingham as Head of the Tactical Air Force but this was rejected. Both Tedder and Portal underlined Park's outstanding ability as a commander set out by *The Times of Malta*'s editorial of 4 January 1944 on his contribution to the defence of the island. There was discussion about Park taking a command in India, which was blocked by Churchill.

During discussions about his future in 1943, Park's old critics reappeared. According to Portal he was not up to standard for a Mediterranean control post because of a lack of skill in the political field. He went further in referring to Park as being 'rather stupid'. His doubts focused on Park as a commander with responsibility outside a purely RAF role. This adverse judgement was not shared by many of those who worked with Park. Certainly Park had to be politically adroit in dealing with partisan movements in Yugoslavia and Greece. Crucially at this stage of the war, where a close relationship with American commanders was vital, the American commanders found Park easier to deal with than many British officers. On the domestic political front, in a skilled move Park arranged to hand over two aircraft to King Farouk before his departure from Egypt. It is an interesting fact that both Tedder and Park were highly rated by the Americans, in contrast to their searing comments about certain Army Generals.

On a personal level, following a degree of persuasion on Park's part, his wife Dol had been able to join him in Cairo. She proved to be an excellent complement to Park with her bright engaging personality and commitment to social welfare, drawing on her previous nursing background.

On 14 January 1944 Park was promoted to become Commander in Chief of the RAF in the Mediterranean and Middle East, taking the place of his old critic Sholto Douglas.

Later that year, his old adversary Leigh-Mallory was killed in a plane crash in the French Alps near Grenoble while flying to India to take up a post as Air Commander in Chief in South East Asia under Mountbatten. He had insisted on flying in bad weather. Park was appointed to replace him and he travelled to the Far East to take up his post on 23 February 1945. The post was to evolve into a largely administrative one, apart from assisting the Allies advance in Burma through the flying in of supplies. His approach to the bureaucracy surrounding a post of this kind was to seek imaginative ways to avoid it. He followed his chosen path of retaining close contact through frequent visits to the men and women under his command.

Chapter 24

Finale as a War Commander

On 23 February 1945 Park took up his Far East command post operating out of headquarters based at Kandy in Ceylon. Under his direction the supply of material reached 2,000 tons a day supporting Slim's army as well as providing fighter cover for the advancing army. During this period in command of the fourteen squadrons Park demonstrated his usual imaginative planning and resourcefulness displaying skill, courage and energy in supporting Allied troops in hostile jungle terrain. The post was characterized by responsibility for forces spread over a vast area, but, as per Uxbridge and Malta, his lean tall figure and pleasant disposition became familiar to many of the men under his charge.

One of his squadron commanders recalls the way in which Sir Keith would 'come over to us at dispersal and would squat down with a muster of pilots around him. Within minutes he would be discussing the minutest details of an operation and displaying an uncanny understanding of our problems. At the same time everybody could ventilate their pet grouch with the sure feeling that if it was possible something would be done to remedy the matter.'

Park had at his disposal in this theatre of the war (often referred to as the 'forgotten campaign' in Britain) an arsenal of American equipment such as B24 bombers, as well as Commonwealth pilots and the support of eight American squadrons. Operating from India and Ceylon a major target was the Burmese capital of Rangoon, but as the fighting strength of the Japanese diminished a major problem became the onset of the monsoon season. In the crucial months of the Allied advance in central Burma the allies' transport crews had the advantage of good weather, but with the coming of the monsoon in May the task of supply became extremely dangerous. To quote Group Captain Isherwood, 'It was more dangerous than any other type of operation. The crews would go out 2 or 3 times daily in violent storms, returning to find their own airfields flooded. Diversion was useless as all the fields were flooded together so that hazardous landings in a sea of mud were a frequent experience.'

Park with his commanders in the Far East.

An advance southwards in Burma meant the added strain of long flights from India not helped by delay in restoring two airfields recently captured from the Japanese. It was not until mid–April 1945 that these airfields were fully operational for transport planes. Park gave credit to the Air Ministry for their agitation to get these airfields operational again. 'Had it not been for the continual pressure from the Air Command it is possible that the development of these bases would have lagged interminably and the supply of forces in central and southern Burma have been insufficient to exploit the victories around Mandalay. It is difficult to describe the urgency and the frequency of these representations that were necessary to awaken the Army to the part they must play in developing an air line of communication.' Park believed that if there had been more urgency in support of the building of airfields and communication systems in Burma the recapture of Burma would have happened earlier.

Park had at his disposal Hurricanes, Spitfires, Beaufighters and Mohawks. His pilots were confronted with the unpalatable prospect that if they were forced down in Japanese-occupied territory and captured they would be brutally treated by the Japanese. As with the Viet Cong in the Vietnam War the Japanese were skilful in hiding their supply routes from the air. Park was at pains to point out even as the end of the war approached that the Japanese remained capable of disrupting the Allies' supply lines and that their Zeros were superior to the aircraft of the Allies.

From Kandy, Park carried out a whole series of inspections, closely examining the physical conditions in which his men were operating. His initial discovery was the paucity of fighter protection available for his fleet of transport aircraft. His usual blunt comment was, 'It seems to me that some of our units pay less attention to the well-being of their men than we did when I was a junior officer.' Meanwhile, Mountbatten commented on Park's report for the BBC: 'The best I have read and quite first class. It has my wholehearted backing against a lack of interest in Britain of the Far East campaign.'

Park continued to retain Beaverbrook's interest and support, as indicated by their frequent correspondence, but he was now operating in an environment dominated by American arms and support. A source of complaint by his men, not of course confined to the Far East, was the higher rates of pay American airmen received.

Before the dropping of the atomic bombs on Hiroshima and Nagasaki which bought the war to an end, the general anticipation was that the war would last for at least another year. On 14 August the Japanese surrendered but not before Park had to communicate to the Foreign Secretary, Anthony Eden, the news that his son had been killed in action. General Slim commented on the role of air support in the Burma campaign: 'Never has an army been better, more unselfishly, or more gallantly supported by an air force.'

After the ceremonial trappings of formal surrender involving Mountbatten, Slim, Lieutenant General Alexander and Park himself, there was the great task of winding down the huge military machine that had waged the war in the Far East. As in Europe, the death camps, the full horror of the suffering of Allied prisoners of war in prison camps throughout the region, was now revealed. The challenge faced by Park and the South East Asia Command (SEAC) administration was to enable the 125,000 victims of the Japanese camps to return to Allied countries as soon as possible. There were insufficient aircraft and ships available to achieve this with the speed that the desperate condition of many of those in the camps demanded together with a reluctance to use Japanese aircraft. Coupled to this was the abrupt cessation of the American lend-lease arrangements which had provided many of the aircraft in SEAC with crucial spares to keep them operational.

In contrast to expectations that Japanese surrender would bring operations to an end, in some parts of the Command they actually increased. This was because the departure of the Japanese was a signal for nationalist movements throughout the region to commence resistance to the return of colonial powers. On the day of the surrender, SEAC found itself responsible for Indochina and the Dutch East Indies, and Park found himself in the invidious position of having to explain to his men why they had to continue to carry out military duties after the war against Japan had concluded.

Chapter 25

No Peace in peacetime

In early 1946 there was a series of mutinies in SEAC. The first of these took place at Mauripur in Karachi when airmen downed tools and refused to work unless their grievances about delays in demobilisation were met. Park was able to avoid treating the stoppages as mutiny because those involved were conscripts rather than professional members of the RAF. The severe penalties around charges for mutiny were thus generally avoided. Other mutinies took place in Ceylon, India and Singapore. In Rangoon the squadron objected to the institution of regular full parades. Park believed that the wing commander concerned should have been aware of how his men felt and reacted accordingly. In Rangoon the mutiny was a result of the men's objection to their poor living conditions. Park had moved to disband 194 Squadron involved in the incident by 15 February 1946.

The air personnel of SEAC lacked many basic amenities, such as razor blades, toothpaste and soap, and were having to forage for them at inflated prices in local domestic markets. In contrast, Americans and Australians serving alongside them enjoyed provision for sports activities, access to books and reading materials, and frequent visits from concert parties. The long-held belief that they were the forgotten campaign was given further stimulus by the inability to improve their conditions following the surrender of the Japanese

A tendency by Park and other leaders in SEAC to blame the unrest which broke out as the work of agitators when rather they needed to focus on the men's grievances was probably misplaced. There was anger with the pace of demobilisation. SEAC had a host of grievances to address but Park's response was to place the blame at the door of the unit commanders for not keeping in sufficient touch with their men. On 26 January 1946 he signalled his commanding officers: 'Investigation has already shown that some commanding officers have not been keeping in close touch with their airmen, especially in regards to explaining the working of the release scheme and investigating complaints about living conditions immediately. Commanding officers should handle complaints tactfully and smoothly. Men should be told to return to work. Commanding officers should remain outwardly calm and good tempered, but every effort is to be made to locate ringleaders, who will be subject to disciplinary action.'

He went on to say that commanding officers should reflect the men's overriding concerns about demobilisation and living conditions by holding parades addressing these at least fortnightly. 'I wish A.O.Cs to report fortnightly by signal that this instruction is being carried out by Commanding Officers,' Park stated. At the same time Park moved ruthlessly to crush any moves to refuse to go on parade. 'When a mass parade is inevitable the Commanding Officer should ensure he has all officers and N.C.Os briefed in preparation to stamp out any open disorder. The RAF Regiment and Service Police should be used on these occasions.'

His determination to root out ringleaders is revealed by his instruction that they must not be shown any leniency up to taking them to court martial. It may be that Park had an exaggerated view of the influence agitators had among the men; there was no easy solution to counter their impatience to return home, no arrangements existed for collective complaint and in post-war Britain no funding to remedy these complaints. It was left to Air Marshal Sir Roderick Carr to provide a more nuanced politically-conscious explanation of why, in countries like India and Indochina, mutinies like those involving hundreds of conscripted men might result in civic disorder with unforeseen consequences.

Park had received an invitation to return to New Zealand on a three-week speaking tour and had written to Tedder requesting his approval. The first paragraph of Tedder's reply readily gave permission for this. 'Not only have you fully deserved recognition from your home country – but also such a visit would be a good thing from the Commonwealth and RAF point of view.' However, what followed from Tedder was reminiscent of the coarse brutality from Air Command that Park had experienced in 1940. 'I must tell you frankly that I can see no prospect of there being any further appointment open to you in the RAF after ACSEA is split up. I rather gathered from your letter that you had not realised this and it is indeed the irony of fate that the duty of telling you this unwelcome news should fall to me – after all our association together and in face of our deep adulation for the magnificent job you have done for the service and for the country. But there it is. Youth must be served.'

Park's response was to write to Mountbatten asking that the acting rank of Air Chief Marshal he held in the post he currently occupied be formally confirmed. Park expressed his 'very great disappointment and shock at being told I will be retired on my return to England. I am quite prepared to be replaced by a younger man but want to protest in the highest quarters if I am asked to retire at a lower rank than Pierce and Garrod and a number of recently promoted Air Chief Marshals. None of these have ever been a Commander in Chief in any theatre. As I have had the good fortune to be associated throughout the 6 years of the War with successful campaigns – Battle of Britain, Malta, Egypt, South East Asia – I do not feel that the treatment suggested by the Air Ministry is just. I hope I can count on your friendly support.'

One explanation for hostility towards Park was his willingness to kick over hornets' nests in defence of the section of the service he served. His report on the campaigns in Burma suggested that the reason for their success was the way in which both the RAF transport support service and its fighter arm operated. He also criticized some of the tactics adopted by the army which brought him into conflict with General Slim. George Pirie, who replaced Park, defended the role played by the RAF in SEAC after Park's departure; he pointed out that in addition to the immensely challenging campaign, they had to cope with the challenge of repatriating the many who had been imprisoned in Japanese prisoner of war camps at conflict end.

Park as a senior commander in the Far East

Park and Sholto Douglas in the Far East.

Park attending surrender ceremonies in the Far East.

Above left: How a cartoonist saw Park.

Above right: Park with his wife Dorothy.

Chapter 26

Post-war Park

*Let me have war say I: It exceeds peace as day does night: it's
sprightly walking and full of vent. Peace is a very apoplexy:
mulled, deaf, sleepy, insensitive: a getter of more bastard children
than war's destroyer of men.*

(Coriolanus Act 4 Scene5).

As always, Shakespeare is available to expose the nub of astute characterization
when required. Like Coriolanus, Park was a man created by the engine of
war. The element of truth in criticisms of Park from men like Portal was
perhaps, like Coriolanus, the absence of some of the skills required of a leader
in peacetime. As the crisis of the mutinies evolved within SEAC a new Park
seemed to appear, making him seem more like a martinet than the Park of the
war years.

Who exactly was Keith Park? Vincent Orange talks about Derek Dowding,
Dowding's son, meeting Park on a number of occasions and always finding
there was a distance in his character it was hard to make contact with. Derek
Dowding had been a Battle of Britain pilot, but even when he ran into him
again in Egypt he met the same austere individual with whom it might be
impossible to confide. That being said, he was unfailingly courteous.

An incident cited by Dr Orange shows Park's approach well. In August
1940 the Hurricane George Westlake was flying suddenly experienced
complete engine failure over the Isle of Wight. He decided to attempt a
landing at Westhampnett. He then failed to see a line of poplars as he taxied
in and collided with them, writing off his plane. On getting back to his base
he was ordered to report to Park. 'How many aircraft have you shot down?'
Park asked. 'One, Sir,' Westlake replied. 'Pity,' Park replied, 'your score is
now exactly zero.' Park then proceeded to upbraid him for not baling out,
trying to force land with his wheels down while having no engine power,
hitting the poplars and generally behaving in an idiotic manner. 'Don't rush

back now but go and read the papers in the mess. I'll be in at lunchtime and you can buy me a beer.' Westlake reports, 'I not only bought him a beer and he bought me a large number, but he asked me to join him for lunch. To this day I can't remember who else was there. As far as I was concerned I could only see the great Keith Park – what a man. From that day I worshipped him.'

Another pilot thought that Park had the characteristics of a bishop, possibly because of his willingness to turn the other cheek as far as Leigh-Mallory was concerned, and his Christian belief. He was not someone for small talk and his personal assistant Wiseman observed that of all those who came to Uxbridge there was no one whom Park would sit down with and chat even for a short time. Wiseman suggested that small talk possibly only happened in the company of his wife and family.

It was Wiseman as well who pointed out Park's impatience with status and the way in which he regarded ground crew and civilian workers as just as important as enlisted members of Fighter Command for its success. Park did not hesitate to pass responsibility down the chain of command particularly with regard to office work although he had the skills for this if necessary.

As he flew around 11 Group he did not hesitate to enter areas of danger. It was through his hands-on experience that he won the respect of the men he led. 'He would say exactly what he meant in perfectly straightforward, loud and clear language and we all had the greatest confidence in him as a leader. To hell with what jealous contemporaries might have thought about him, he was OUR boy all right,' Michael Crossley, a top pilot, commented.

There is nothing in Park's history to suggest that he ever departed from the conventional viewpoint of who were the enemy. He variously refers to the Germans, Italians and Japanese with phrases such as 'Huns' and 'Japs'. Dr Orange refers to his strong Christian beliefs, but apart from the adoption of orthodox Church of England attitudes it is difficult to detect anything in his life that manifested a strong Christian faith. His personal assistant at Uxbridge suggested that Park had once confessed that he would have been happy to have had a career in the Anglican Church.

He appeared to have no qualms about leaving the New Zealand Army on Gallipoli and joining the artillery section of the Imperial Army in 1915. This led to his fighting on the Somme in the following year before he joined the Royal Flying Corps. Like many of his generation he thought the fate of New Zealand was synonymous with that of Britain, hence the New Zealand Prime Minister's statement after the British declaration of war in 1939: 'Where Britain goes we go.' Yet as the character of the war changed and the result came to depend increasingly on the Americans, Park was outstanding in the effective way he was able to work with Eisenhower in the Mediterranean. This might well have arisen because unlike some British commanders he did not carry the baggage of social class. Perhaps more importantly Park was more akin to an American commander in the way he dealt with the mechanics of military command and his openness to new technology and fresh approaches – witness the way he insisted on going onto the offensive when he took over in 1942 in Malta. A greater insight into Park's psychology would likely have been revealed if he had written an autobiography after coming out of hospital in 1946 as he promised.

Awaiting Park in 1946 was news of his son Colin's court martial on 3 August. It appeared in the evidence that he had driven out of the Möhnesee Club towards Nauheim in Germany in an armoured car with John Armstrong of the 11th Hussars. Park, of the Black Watch, and Armstrong, had fired the gun on their vehicle in what they said was empty countryside. Unfortunately the shell killed 10-year-old Andreas Noterski who was approaching them on the other side of the road. A court martial was convened and both men were found guilty of manslaughter on the basis that they had been drinking and that their behaviour was irresponsible.

There would be other domestic tragedies in Park's life. On 3 September 1951 his youngest son Ian was killed while serving with the Perak Aboriginal Constabulary following an ambush on the Perak River in Malaysia. Vincent

Orange comments about how Park's wife Dorothy never really recovered from news of his death when it reached them in New Zealand, although Park's response was more sanguine, squaring his shoulders and getting on with life.

It was 31 years since he had been in New Zealand and Dol had never visited the country before. Park nursed an ambition of going into business in his retirement. He first returned to Argentina as a base to work as a trade

Park at the end of the war.

ambassador in South America for the Hawker Siddeley Company. Great importance was attached to his work with the Perón government promoting the sale of British aircraft to the Argentinians because of the desperate state of the British post-war economy. However, as others have found, his sales activity was in direct competition with American interests and at each stage had to be cleared by the American administration. Further, after fighting a war against fascist regimes the crude dictatorship of Perón hardly represented a regime suitable for the sale of military aircraft. Park may have been aware that Argentina was opening its borders to escaping war criminals from Germany and some of the states occupied by the Nazis but there is no indication that this limited his sales activities.

Then an opportunity arose on his return to New Zealand to work as Hawker Siddeley representative in the Pacific and by 1948 he was in Auckland becoming a City Councillor. In April 1958 Dowding contacted Park about the closure of his operations room at Uxbridge. He had unveiled a plaque to mark Park's association. For the last time the operations room was in use and the operations table again showed the reaction to raids that occurred on 15 September 1940. The only surviving Hurricane and Spitfire flew overhead. Warrant Officer Leonard Lyons, the map supervisor, recalled how Park would join them in the control room after the Battle was over: 'He was very friendly with everyone and rank was nothing to him.'

Lord Willoughby de Broke, the senior controller at Uxbridge, was someone else who contacted Park about the memorial event. He recalled that years had passed since they last met, but 'Friendship came to mind so vividly and heard on all sides were expressions of regret that Park was not present.' He went on to say: 'One of my most treasured possessions is the copy of your 11 Group Dispatch which you so kindly sent me when you gave up command of the Group and retired to the Air Ministry.'

In 1970 the distinguished New Zealand fighter ace Alan Deere produced a study of the tactics that were employed during the Battle of Britain. His careful analysis suggested support for the way Park had managed the battle. He sent it to Slessor saying, 'I like to think that if I'd been in Stuffy's [Dowding's] place I would have much earlier told Leigh-Mallory to shut up and get on with commanding his Group … To my mind it was intolerable that a C-in-C should have been subject to it – and I was there and heard the whole thing. Keith Park (another rather difficult customer I'm afraid) was first class throughout and it put him in a very difficult position. He was an extremely good Fighter AOC – as he proved again in Malta later – but I'm afraid that was his upper limit.'

Others did not agree that Park was of limited ability. Sir Kenneth Porter, who was at Park's morning briefings at Uxbridge to his heads of department, remembered how he never needed to spell out issues arising in great detail because Park was always ahead of him and seemed to have a complete picture of the issue that had been raised although he was not trained in signals. He admitted that Park was not particularly friendly and lived completely for his Command. There was an element of ruthlessness to him and he had no compunction about dispatching anyone not measuring up to his standards (an example of this is revealed by a comment by two officers on learning Park would take control on Malta who had met Park's disapproval: 'Well that's us being transferred.' Two days later they received notice of their transfer).

A distinctive feature of Park was the way he never set himself apart from those working around him. He made extensive use of the telephone and would appear unannounced anywhere in his Group. Porter who was aware that Park was a beneficiary of Ultra information felt that this was supplemented by a shrewd appraisal of German actions.

Porter was someone who knew Leigh-Mallory as well as Park and therefore was able to evaluate them both. He thought that Leigh-Mallory was only outstanding with regard to his pomposity and was preoccupied with appearances. Despite his pre-war experience he conspicuously lacked Park's hands-on character.

Now back in New Zealand was the man who for a few months in 1940 held the future of civilisation in his hands as the RAF fought a desperate rearguard action against the all-conquering Luftwaffe. Although initially hailed and greeted as a hero, there were always going to be difficulties coming to terms with a society of about two million citizens far removed from the stresses of a World War. Speaking to a large reception in Dunedin Town Hall he said, 'I have been looking forward to coming back to my native land, but never in my wildest dreams did I expect such a regal reception.' An interesting parallel perhaps with Sir Leslie Monroe, the former President of the United Nations General Assembly, who came to be referred to as 'Sir Leslie name drop', the consequence of having to exist in a parochial environment.

Ahead of him was work as an Auckland City Councillor and unfortunately Dol's protracted illness. Orange suggests that it was not his colonial origins that prevented Park from going right to the top, although looking through the times he was passed over or had to fight for valid recognition this seems to have played some part. One factor was that he was not particularly clubbable and did not easily make close friends. Orange suggests that high command were the losers not having Park to mastermind air support for D-Day and the Normandy invasion or an air force in a post-war environment.

Air Marshal Sir Keith Park died in Auckland Hospital on 2 February 1975, and on 12 September 1975, Sir Douglas Bader, who had been so active in his criticism in 1940, was invited to give his eulogy at St. Clement Danes Church in The Strand. Bader said: 'The awesome responsibility for the country's survival rested squarely on Sir Keith Park's shoulders, the man whose memory we honour today. Had he failed, 'Stuffy' Dowding's foresight, determination and achievement would have counted for nought. This is no sad occasion. Rather it is a time when we can let our memories drift back to those halcyon days of 1940 when we fought together in English skies under

Above: Park re-enters the business world in New Zealand.

Right: Unveiling statue of Park in London in 2009

AIR CHIEF MARSHAL
SIR KEITH PARK
GCB KBE MC & BAR DFC DCL MA RAF
1892 - 1975

Park in Auckland outside his house with his wife.

the determined leadership of that great New Zealander we are remembering now... Keith Park was one of us. We all shared the great experience. That is what we remember today. British military history has been enriched with the names of great fighting men from New Zealand of all ranks and in every one of our services. Keith Park's name is carved into that history alongside those of his peers.'

In 2009, the then Mayor of London, Boris Johnson, unveiled a statue in Waterloo Place to the memory of Keith Park. A bust stands too at the Battle of Britain Memorial site on the white cliffs near Dover. These tributes do perhaps suggest that the shoddy treatment afforded to Park after his huge contribution to success in the Battle of Britain had to some extent been rectified. I can only say after my research for this book, that it was not before time.

Bibliography

Allen, H.R., DFC, *Who Won the Battle of Britain?*, Arthur Barker 1974

Avery, Max and Shores, Christopher, *Spitfire Leader: Flying Career of Wing Commander Evan (Rosie) Mackie, DSO, DFC and Bar, DFC(US), New Zealand Fighter Ace*, Grub Street 1997

Battle of Britain – An Air Ministry Account of the Great Days from 8th August – 31st October 1940, HMSO London 1941

Bergström, Christer, *Battle of Britain – The Epic Conflict Revisited*, Casemate, 2015

Bickers, Richard Townshend, *Battle of Britain*, Salamander 1990

Bowman, Martin W., *Duxford and the Big Wings*, Pen and Sword 2009

Bowyer, Michael, *2 Group RAF – A Complete History 1936–1945*, Faber and Faber 1974

Bowyer, Michael, *Battle of Britain*, Patrick Stephens 2010

Brickhill, Paul, *Reach for the Sky*, Collins 1954

Brittan, Vera, *England's Hour*, Bloomsbury 2005

Brooks, Robin, *Aerodromes of Fighter Command – Then and Now*, After the Battle 2014

Brown, Hamish, *Wine, Women and Song – A Spitfire Pilot's Story*, Fonthill 2012.

Brown, Squadron Leader Peter, *Honour Restored*, The History Press 2005

Buckton, Henry, *An Illustrated Introduction to the Battle of Britain*, Amberley 2015

Buckton, Henry, *Voices from the Battle of Britain: Surviving Veterans tell their Story*, David and Charles 2010

Bungay, Stephen, *The Most Dangerous Enemy – A History of The Battle of Britain*, Aurum 2000

Churchill, W.S., *History of the Second World War, (Vol.2 Their Finest Hour)*, Cassell 1949

Claasen, Adam, *Dogfight: The Battle of Britain*, Pen and Sword 2012

Collier, Richard, *Eagle Day – The Battle of Britain*, Hodder and Stoughton 1966

Cotter, Jerod, *Battle of Britain Memorial Flight: 50 Years of Flying*, Pen and Sword 2007

Cull, Brian and Gulea, Frederick, *Spitfires Over Malta: The Epic Air Battles of 1942*, Grub Street 2005

Deere, Alan, *Nine Lives*, Crecy 1999

Deighton, Len, *Battle of Britain*, Jonathan Cape 1980

Dixon, J.E.G., *Dowding and Churchill*, Pen and Sword 2008

Donahue, Art, *Life as a Battle of Britain Spitfire Pilot*, Amberley 2010

Flint, Peter, *Dowding and Headquarters Fighter Command*, Airlife 1996

Franks, Norman, *Air Battle for Dunkirk*, William Kimber (1983)

Franks, Norman, *Dowding's Eagles*, Pen and Sword Aviation 2015

Franks, Norman, *RAF Fighter Command*, Patrick Stevens 1992

Frayne Turner, John, *The Bader Wing*, Turner Midian 1981

Frayne Turner, John, *The Battle of Britain*, BCA 1990

Freeman, John, *Battle of Britain –The Forgotten Masters*, Air Record, 1998

Glancey, Jonathan, *Spitfire*, Atlantic 2006

Gretzyngier, Robert, *Poles in Defence of Britain*, Grub Street 2001

Hall, Roger, *Clouds of Fear*, Bailey Brothers 1975

Holland, James, *Battle of Britain*, Corgi 2010

Holmes, Tony, *Hurricane Aces 1939-40*, Osprey 1998

Isby, David, *Decisive Duel: Spitfire vs 109*, Little, Brown 2012

Kaplan, Philip, *Fighter Aces of the RAF in the Battle of Britain*, Pen and Sword 2007

Korda, Michael, *With Wings like Eagles*, JR 2009

Lake, Jon, *Battle of Britain*, Silverdale Books 2000

Mason, Francis, *Hawker Hurricane*, Acton 1987

McDonald, Paul, *Malta's Greater Siege & Adrian Warburton*, Pen and Sword 2015

McKay, Sinclair, *Fighter Command – The Men and Women who beat the Luftwaffe*, Aurum 2015

McKay, Sinclair, *The Secret Life of Fighter Command*, Aurum 2015

McKinstry, Leo, *Hurricane: Victor of The Battle of Britain*, John Murray 2011

McKinstry, Leo, *Spitfire: Portrait of a Legend*, John Murray 2007

Milton, Brian, *Hurricane: The Last Witnesses*, André Deutsch 2010

Nesbit, Roy Convers, *Battle of Britain*, History Press 2000

BIBLIOGRAPHY

Newton Dunn, Bill, *Big Wing: The Biography of Air Chief Marshal Sir Trafford Leigh-Mallory, KCB, DSO and Bar*, Airlife 1992

Nichols, Steve, *Malta Spitfire Aces*, Osprey 2008

Oliver, David, *Fighter Command: 1939-45*, Harper Collins 2000

Orange, Vincent, *Sir Keith Park*, Methuen 1984

Parker, Matthew, *The Battle of Britain July – October 1940*, Headline 2000

Price, Alfred, *Battle of Britain – The Hardest Day*, Gale Cengage 1988

Price, Alfred, *Spitfire Combat*, Southern 2003

Probert, Air Commodore Henry, and Cox, Sebastian, *The Battle Re-Thought*, RAF Historical Society 1990

Richards, Denis and Hough, Richard, *Battle of Britain*, Pen and Sword 1989

Rogers, Anthony, (ed.), *185 The Malta Squadron*, Spellmount 2015

Ross, David, *Richard Hillary*, Grub Street 2000

Sarkar, Dilip, *Last of the Few*, Amberley 2010

Sarkar, Dilip, *The Few*, Amberley 2009

Shores, Christopher; Cull, Brian; Malizia, Nicola, *Malta: The Hurricane Years 1940-41*, Grub Street 1987

Simpson, Geoff, *A Dictionary of the Battle of Britain: In Association with the Battle of Britain Memorial Trust*, Halsgrove 2009

Smith, N.D., *Battle of Britain*, Faber 1962

Sutherland, Jon, and Canwell, Diane, *Air War Malta: June 1940 to November 1942*, Pen and Sword 2008

Sutton, Barry, *Fighter Boy*, Amberley 2010

Taylor, A.J.P., *English History 1914-1945*, OUP 1965

Tracy, David, *Rise and Fall of the Luftwaffe*, Weidenfeld and Nicolson 1973

Wellum, Geoffrey, *First Light*, Viking 2002

Index